DOUBLE DOWN ON YOUR DATA

Qualex Consulting Services, Inc
4300 Biscayne Bay, Suite 203
Miami, FL 33137.
www.qlx.com

Copyright © 2009 Clive J. Pearson. All rights reserved.

No part of this book may be reproduced, stored in a retrieval system, or transmitted by any means without the written permission of the author, excepting brief quotes used in reviews.

First published by Qualex Consulting Services on 3/10/09.

First Printing: March 2009

Printed in the United States of America.

This book is printed on acid-free paper.

Cataloging data may be obtained from the Library of Congress

ISBN 978-0-615-28489-7

DOUBLE DOWN ON YOUR DATA

How analytics is revolutionizing the casino industry

by

Clive J. Pearson

TABLE OF CONTENTS

ACKNOWLEDGEMENT 1
INTRODUCTION 3
CHAPTER ONE 9
    CUSTOMER RELATIONSHIP MANAGEMENT 9
        Overview 9
        Customer Relationship Management 10
        Player Tracking 13
        Data Integration 15
        Data Mining: An In-House Goldmine 15
        Predictive Analytics: Actionable Intelligence 18
        Increase Customer Value 19
        Up-sell and cross-sell 20
        Pearl River Resort: A Case Study 20
        Conclusion 22

CHAPTER TWO 25
    THE INDUSTRY'S CURRENT STANDARD 25
        Overview 25
        Property Management System 25
        Point-of-Sales Systems (POS) 26
        Graphic User Interface (GUI) Requirements 27
        Agilysys 28
        Aristocrat 28
        Bally 30
        IGT Advantage System 31
        Kronos 32
        Micros OPERA 33
        Conclusion 34

CHAPTER THREE 37
    CASINO MARKETING 37
        Overview 37
        Market Segmentation 38
        Marketing Cycle and Demand Creation 40
        Marketing Campaigns 41
        Automating and Streamlining the Campaign Processes 41
        Predictive Modeling 42
        Campaign Effectiveness: Capturing Response Data 43
        Social Networking and Microblogs: Valuable Unfiltered Information 44
        Conclusion 45

CHAPTER FOUR ... 49

MOBILE-IZE YOUR MARKETING: THE VIRAL IMPACT ... 49
Overview ... 49
Mobile Marketing: Endless Options ... 52
Picture Messaging and Bar Codes ... 54
Mobile Loyalty ... 55
Mobile Analytics ... 56
Conclusion ... 57

CHAPTER FIVE ... 59

RADIO FREQUENCY IDENTIFICATION ... 59
Overview ... 59
How It Works ... 60
Monitoring Play ... 62
Card Counters: Count Them out ... 62
Theft and Counterfeit ... 64
Responsible Gaming ... 65
Beyond Chips: A Different Smart Card ... 65
Conclusion ... 66

CHAPTER SIX ... 69

TABLE-GAMES REVENUE MANAGEMENT ... 69
Overview ... 69
Table-Games Revenue Management (TGRM): Demand Based Pricing ... 70
Conclusion ... 73

CHAPTER SEVEN ... 75

THE CASINO FLOOR: A BRAVE NEW WORLD ... 75
Overview ... 75
A 24-Hour Sports Book ... 76
Mobile Check-In ... 76
Marketing at the Slot Machine ... 77
No More Standing In Line For a Table ... 78
Server Based Gaming ... 78
Slot Search ... 78
Conclusion ... 79

CHAPTER EIGHT ... 81

THE ASIAN GAMBLER ... 81
Overview ... 81
Rolling Chip Programs ... 82
Chinese Gambling Dos and Don'ts ... 83
Asian Games ... 84
Conclusion ... 86

CHAPTER NINE 89
    A COMPREHENSIVE SOLUTION 89
        Overview 89
        Patron Data Quality and Integration 90
        Patron Value 91
        Patron Segmentation 91
        Patron Predictive Modeling 91
        Patron Revenue Forecasting 92
        Total Guest View 92
        Guest Intelligence 92
        Query & Analysis 94
        OLAP Analysis 94
        Visualization 95
        Integrated Analytics 95
        Deliverables 95
        Internet Gambling 97
        Conclusion 98
GLOSSARY 101
REFERENCES 107
ABOUT THE AUTHOR 111
        Clive Pearson *111*
INDEX 113

ACKNOWLEDGEMENT

First and foremost I would like to thank my editor, Andrew Pearson, who assisted me by reading several early drafts and was also instrumental in correcting proofs. He even came up with a few interesting anecdotes about the history of gambling, which added a lot of color to the manuscript. I would also like to thank the members of the Qualex gaming practice, specifically John Enriquez and Steve Wagar.

INTRODUCTION

Gambling — the wagering of money or something of material value on an event with an uncertain outcome with the primary intent of winning additional money and/or material goods — has been with us since ancient times. Greek mythology tells the story of Poseidon, Zeus and Hades dividing the world between them in a dice game; Poseidon won the sea, Zeus the heavens and Hades the underworld. The land, I guess, was left to the rest of us. During the Trojan War, Homer writes that the mythological hero Palamedes — who is credited with inventing the dice — created games of chance to entertain his troops. The ancient Egyptians, Persians, Indians and Chinese all played games of chance, some with lethal consequences. From these intriguing beginnings have arisen the opulent gambling temples of today; the Bellagio, Luxor and Monte Carlos of Las Vegas; the Taj Mahal, the Tropicana and Caesars of Atlantic City; and the Babylon, the Mandarin Oriental and the Grand Emperor of Macau. Gambling unites peoples as diverse as the ancient Romans, the Mesopotamian Persians, the 7th Century Chinese, the Medieval Europeans and the modern day Americans.

Gambling has, of course, changed dramatically since those ancient times. Today's casino operators are faced with a gambler who is much more sophisticated than the ancient Roman soldier who tossed a coin in the air and called "Heads or Ships[1]." To succeed in today's highly competitive world, casino operators must understand their customers like never before. Luckily for them, we have entered a brave new world of gambling and entertainment where customers knowingly — and oftentimes unknowingly

---

[1] Roman coins had the head of the God Janus on one side and a Roman galley on the opposite side.

— leave clues to their gambling behavior. Predictive analytics allow casino operators to quantify every dollar a customer spends in the casino. This is data that can be used to not only predict the customer's unique value to the property but it also provides clues that will make marketing campaigns directed to that individual much more effective.

Long ago, casino operators understood the importance of analytics. They knew that, since as little as one percent of overall casino customers can drive as much as 20 percent of a company's revenue, it is imperative to know who these patrons are and how best to market to them. This book was written to show casino management how to best cull through their in-house patron data to discover who their most profitable patrons are.

It is the hope of this writer that, after reading this book, the reader will come away with an understanding of all of the current tools available to casino operators, tools that can help them better manage their patron's experiences. In this rapidly changing business environment, where the average casino patron is no longer loyal to just one particular casino, it is imperative for casino operators to understand the habits of their patrons so that they can effectively market to them. Once the casino operator has successfully enticed the patron onto their property, they must ensure that nothing gets in the way of his or her entertainment, whether that entertainment is gambling or one of the many other non-gambling activities offered by the casino property.

Today's casino landscape is a far cry from what it was just twenty short years ago. The theme-oriented casinos and resorts of yesterday have given way to slick upscale hotels that are targeting a more adult and more sophisticated customer. With its shrewdly rebellious slogan 'What happens in Vegas stays in Vegas,' Las Vegas is deemphasizing its family friendly past and focusing on a more mature future. As with other service industries, casino operators are faced with an inherent problem — how do I differentiate myself from my competitors when the tools I have at my disposal are basically exactly the same as what my competitors have. After all, a blackjack table at the Venetian is exactly the same as a blackjack table at the Hard Rock Casino. The answer lies in customer experience. A casino has to be smarter than its competitors in attracting its customers and then marketing to them.

In chapter four, I discuss mobile marketing and the enormous potential SMS text marketing has for casino operators. This powerful and highly cost-effective, direct marketing tool should be a part of every casino's marketing plan as it not only offers great marketing potential but it also has the unique ability of being the endpoint in a casino's revenue management system. A casino can instantly connect to a consumer with offers that can help the casino fill seats at a table, in a concert hall, or even increase turnout at a bar or nightclub, thereby increasing revenue and selling seats that would otherwise have gone unused.

Chapter five deals with Radio Frequency Identification (RFID) technology, which has been implemented in several casinos, including The Wynn in Las Vegas. It allows for real-time monitoring of chip inventory and instant chip validation. It can also let a user know the entire history of each casino chip throughout its lifetime. This function allows casino operators to create a very accurate picture of a player's gambling habits — what games he plays, how high his stakes are, and how he tips, among other things. This precise information allows the casino to divvy out their comps more accurately when compared to the patron's real spend.

Chapter six shows how a casino operator can couple their RFID technology with a table-games revenue management system that gives them a very accurate picture of capacity and supply and therefore shows them how to manipulate table wager minimums with more precision, which should results in increased table games revenue.

The Internet revolution has been a consumer revolution more than anything else. With it came a shift in power from manufacturers, suppliers, advertisers and businesses to the consumer. The vast amount of information available to the consumer almost forces companies to be transparent about their operations. The wrath of the consumer can be swift and lethal. Today's business executives know full well that they are only a mouse click away from an irate customer and that one disgruntled customer's wrath can circumnavigate the globe in seconds, which can cause other customers to immediately reject their products or services. What the customer gains in transparency, however, they lose in privacy. Smart executives have learned how to cull through their customer data and analyze it to predict behavioral patterns. Marketing to those behavioral patterns can prove irresistible to the customer and, therefore, drive revenue straight to the company's bottom line.

I conclude this book with a description of an ideal solution that gives casino managers a clear understanding of their patrons. A solution designed to support hotel and resort operational departments with one clean and complete view of the guest. This solution combines all of the casino patron's activity — not only the amount of money the customer gambles on the casino floor but also how much they spend on everything else at the resort, including such expenses as food and retail, sporting activities, water park or spa visits, among many other things. Armed with this valuable knowledge, casinos can easily understand who their most profitable customers are and then develop laser-focused marketing campaigns that will specifically appeal to those individuals.

Working in tandem with a casino's Property Management System, this solution allows casino management to track each patron's individual gaming habits, which in turn helps determine who the casino's most valuable players are. Casino marketing departments find this information instrumental when deciding who they should market to and what promotions are the most likely to find success. Instead of taking a scatter-shot approach to marketing, a casino can laser-focus their marketing campaigns, thereby getting the most out of their marketing dollars. After all, it sometimes makes sense for a casino to choose a non-gambling patron over a gambler if that patron adds more to the bottom line.

Gambling has been with us since ancient times and will undoubtedly be with us forever; it's just too much a part of our culture, especially we Americans. After all, our country was founded on men and women who put their names into a lottery for the chance at a new — and hopefully better — life in an unknown country. And who doesn't enjoy the thrill of placing a wager on some unexpected event? Most gamblers would agree with Paul Newman's character Fast Eddie Felson in the film *The Color of Money* when he says, "Money won is twice as sweet as money earned." Perhaps there's a touch of irony in the fact that casino operators now use analytics and probability theory to increase their business. After all, one of the founding fathers of probability theory — Blaise Pascal — was asked by gamblers to solve the practical problem of how to divide the take when a game of cards was interrupted because an aristocrat had to leave the table (Reith, 2002). No matter how desperately a government attempts to stifle it, the gambling industry is here to stay. It is the goal of this author to help casino operators achieve a new level of patron experience.

CHAPTER ONE

CUSTOMER RELATIONSHIP MANAGEMENT

> *"The easiest kind of relationship is with ten thousand people, the hardest is with one."*
> ~Joan Baez

Overview

There is an old adage in marketing circles that says it is far more cost effective to keep a customer than to get a new one. On average, it takes five times as much time and money to find a new customer than it does to retain a customer you already have. Today's casino operators are taking this philosophy very much to heart. Few industries are as reliant on computers and software as the casino business. Although at first reluctant to embrace computer technology, casino operators quickly realized that they could not exist without them. Checking in thousands of guests on a nightly basis would be impossible without a computerized hotel system. A majority of casinos now run more than 200 computer applications, everything from a property management system, to slot player tracking software, to communication systems, to security systems, to entertainment ticketing systems, to backup power systems, and many things in-between. Keeping all of this data under control and communicating with each other is a massive undertaking. To succeed, casino operators must have good answers to the following questions:

- How can we get our most profitable customers into our casino?
- How can we anticipate our customer's needs?

- How can we enhance our customer's experience and thereby maximize our profitability?
- How can we provide the right offer to the right customer at the right time and at the right price?
- How can we retain our existing customers while also acquiring new ones?
- What is the best marketing strategy to entice our customers to return to the casino not only to gamble but also to utilize our resort's full suite of services?
- How can we take market share away from our competitors?

The answer to all of these questions lies in Customer Relationship Management.

Customer Relationship Management

Customer Relationship Management (CRM) is a strategy used to learn more about a customer's needs and behaviors in order to develop stronger relationships with them and thereby create a value exchange on both sides. Also known as Customer Loyalty Programs, CRM is a two-part process; firstly, it is the method by which a company tracks and organizes its current and prospective customers; secondly, it is the process by which a company manages the endpoints of customer relationships through its marketing promotions. The history of the casino industry is filled with examples of CRM initiatives that although expensive to implement did little more than the systems they replaced or, because of one reason or another, they simply failed miserably. CRM should enable data to be converted into information that provides insight into customer behavior in all areas of the casino property or across properties, thereby enabling casino operators to measure the total value of the customer.

The rise in popularity and the rapid growth of the gaming industry has created a highly competitive environment for all casino properties. Industry-leading gaming companies have expressed the need to identify and develop their clientele so as to enhance the guest experience as well as to increase customer loyalty and to generate new business. This can be achieved using Business Intelligence (BI) and CRM solutions to provide greater property and guest intelligence by delivering a total and comprehensive guest view. CRM allows companies to:

- Leverage the full range of their overall property data to better understand guest preferences in the following areas:
    - Slots
    - Player Cards
    - Table Games
    - Hospitality
    - Food and Beverage
    - Retail and Entertainment
    - Marketing Promotions
- Gain greater guest intelligence for more individualized customer communications and touch points.
- Pinpoint influencers on player behavior to drive greater gaming revenue.

- Maximize the total guest value by attracting and retaining customers with the greatest propensity to be profitable over their lifetime.
- Realize the effectiveness of the properties various promotions and marketing campaigns.
- Forecast the future value of guest activity and project property revenue streams based on advanced analytic techniques.
- Understand how guest spend and gaming activity, promotions, and hotel fill rates affect the property's financial bottom line.

All of this information can empower a casino operator to deliver a gaming and hospitality experience that will make its customers feel important and well served. Additionally, it will allow casino executives to make better and more informed decision about their guests and their properties.

With this information, casino operators can develop a true value for each guest, a value that combines transactions from each operational system, whether those systems are player tracking, slots, table games, hotel, point-of-sale, retail, and food and beverage. This unified view of the guest incorporates information from all touch points and channels, ensuring that customer information is consistent, secure, accurate and understandable to all users.

Player Tracking

Free to join, frequent player programs are usually credit-based loyalty programs that reward customers for their play and entertainment choices. The rewards, which can include free or discounted rooms, meals, shows, sporting activities or even priority check-in, are based on how much the patron plays, what types of games they play, and how much they spend on other activities at the casino property. They are generally based on a tier system, meaning patrons work their way up to higher levels of rewards; for example, Harrah's Total Rewards program has three levels — Gold, Platinum and Diamond. The over-riding philosophy of these programs is to reward casino patrons for their play and entertainment spend. These programs are instrumental for casino operators to gain insight into their patrons. Much of the analytic data that this book discusses comes from the personalized data in these rewards programs. It's an enormous amount of data. Harrah's Total Rewards program alone has more than 30 million members[2].

The program rewards are based upon what's known as the player's Theoretical Win or Theo for short. The theoretical win represents what is supposed to happen, while the actual win/loss represents what actually did happen with respect to a particular player's gaming activity. If the casino only takes into consideration theoretical win, then they may lose profitable players who have had a big loss, while if they only consider the actual win, then they may have difficulty maintaining profits in the long run, given the escrow effect or the difference between theoretical and actual. In general, the calculation of the theoretical win is handled automatically within the

---

[2] http://promomagazine.com/incentives/harrahs_caesarsmembers_072005/index.html (accessed March 1, 2009).

player management system and is pretty standard within the industry. The basic calculation is:

Theoretical Win = Average Bet x Hours Played x Decisions per Hour x House Advantage (Kilby and Fox, 1998).

The house advantage is the statistical advantage the casino has over the player. These advantages differ according to the game played. For example, suppose a baccarat player bets $500 per hand for 12 hours at 60 hands per hour. Using a house advantage of 1.2%, this player's worth to the casino is $4,320.00 ($500 x 12 x 60 x 1.2%).

In addition to the theoretical and actual win amounts for a player session, the player management system also calculates the comp[3] and point values earned for that session. The system also gathers and records information such as the time and date when the session started, which slot machine or table the patron played on, as well as how long the session lasted.

In summary, player-tracking is one of the most important tools a casino has to determine who its most valuable players are. This information helps management determine which players deserve a comp and how much the comp should be worth. The player tracking data is the single most important source of information for the casino's marketing efforts.

---

[3] Comp - a free item the casino provides to players based on their play.

Data Integration

Over the past decade, casino patrons have become more sophisticated than ever before. Now, it's abundantly clear that, like everybody else, casino patrons are more likely to respond to offers that are tailored specifically for them. By understanding what type of patron is at their property, why they are there, and what they like to do while they are there (i.e., do they like to gamble, go to the spa, join the long line at the buffet or prefer the property's high-end restaurants), casino operators can individualize their marketing campaigns so that these campaigns are more likely to be effective. With analytics, casino operators can even predict which low-tier and mid-tier customers are likely to become the next "high rollers." In so doing, casinos can afford to be more generous in their offers as they know that there is a high likelihood that these customers will appreciate the personalized attention and therefore become long term — and, hopefully, highly profitable — patrons.

Data Mining: An In-House Goldmine

Once casino operators have accumulated all of this customer data they are then faced with the problem of how best to analyze it and this is where data mining — the process whereby hidden patterns are discovered within data sets — comes in. Data mining helps transform raw data into usable information. By employing automated predictive analytics to sift through a casino operator's customer database, data mining can discover hidden opportunities and connections that would otherwise have gone unnoticed. Many casino operators have terabytes and terabytes of data — everything from customer player card information to information about a customer's room preference — and sifting through this information to discover meaningful connections would be an impossible task without data mining.

Data mining culls through the data from such disparate sources and departments as sales, credit, and marketing and allows users to measure patron behavior on more than a hundred different attributes, which is a far cry from the three or four different attributes that statistical modeling used to offer. Included in the most common techniques are:

- **Artificial neural networks**: A mathematical model based on biological neural networks.
- **Decision trees**: Used to identify the strategy that is most likely to reach a goal. It is a decision support tool that uses a graph or model of decisions and their possible consequences, including chance event outcomes, resource costs, and utility.
- **Genetic algorithms**: A search technique that uses genetic combinations, mutation, inheritance, selection and crossover to find exact or approximate solutions to optimization and search problems.
- **Nearest neighbor method**: An optimization problem for finding closest points in metric spaces.
- **Rule induction**: An area of machine learning in which formal rules are extracted from a set of observations.

Unlike traditional statistical analysis, which relies heavily on hypothesis testing, data mining tries to identify relationships and interdependencies that affect a marketing-related opportunity or problem (Thelen, et al., 2004). While traditional multiple regression methods can only use a limited number of complexity levels, neural networks and decision trees can easily handle up to 200 predictor variables (Thelen, et al., 2004).

Normally, with statistical modeling, an analyst poses a simple question such as: "Are higher-income people prone to be more loyal to a casino player card than those with lower income levels?" The hypothesis would elicit two responses, either "yes" or "no." Data mining, however, can reveal factors that contribute to casino loyalty; factors that the analyst might never have been testing for. In general, the data mining process is as follows:

1. Identify the business opportunity
2. Cleanse the data
3. Transform the data into meaningful information
4. Confirm the model
5. Tweak and perfect the model (Thelen, et al., 2004).

Data mining systems are inherently reliant on so many departments therefore they can be complicated to implement. Marketing managers, corporate strategists, statisticians and IT directors are all required to add their input. Casino operators should keep in mind, however, that data mining would only be successful if their casino patrons are willing to provide information on themselves (Thelen, et al., 2004). Although player cards provide a wealth of information, if the patron doesn't trust the casino with information beyond what is gleaned from the player cards the casino will only have a limited view of their individual patrons.

Predictive Analytics: Actionable Intelligence

Customer analytics have evolved from simply reporting patron behavior to segmenting customers based on profitability, to predicting that profitability, to improving those predictions because of the inclusion of new data, to manipulating customer behavior with target-specific promotional offers and marketing campaigns. Predictive analytics can develop a customer's value over time as well as predict that customer's behavior. From these analytics, a casino operator can tailor highly specific, laser-focused marketing campaigns to each customer in the casino's patron database. By consolidating the various patron touch point systems throughout the casino property, the casino operator can create a full view of each of their patron.

Drawing on data from casino player cards, predictive models can set budgets and calendars for gamblers, calculating their predicted lifetime value. If a gambler wagers less than usual because they may have skipped a monthly visit the casino can intervene with a letter or a phone call offering a free meal, a show ticket or cash vouchers. Without these analytics, casino operators might not notice a slight, almost imperceptible change in customer behavior that portends problems. For example, if a long-time customer decides to cash in all their player card points perhaps it's because they are dissatisfied with their last experience at the casino. Predictive analytics can quickly spot these trends and alert casino management to the issue so that they can approach the individual to find out if there is a problem. This kind of personalized attention can go a long way in appeasing disgruntled customers, which might help retain them.

Predictive analytics can glean data from a variety of different sources, including:

- Data integration from all gaming systems;
- Feedback information derived from telemarketing the guests or other post-visit surveys;
- Web data mining from customer's individual online behavior.

With predictive analytics, gaming organizations can easily segment their customers and coordinate marketing campaigns to effectively target each segment across each outbound channel. For example, if a casino customer is scheduled to receive all of his event promotions via e-mail, the predictive analytics solution will automatically remove him from concurrent campaigns being run through other channels. This ensures consistency and also improves customer satisfaction, since the organization respects the customer's contact preference and doesn't inundate him with multiple offers. Moreover, a predictive analytics solution monitors channel capacity and usage to eliminate overload and distribute campaigns equally across channels. If one channel is at risk of overload, the solution automatically shifts the remainder of a campaign to a different channel to ensure completion. This enables organizations to maximize the capacity and value of each channel without resorting to time-consuming manual monitoring.

Increase Customer Value

Since as little as one percent of overall customers can drive as much as 20 percent of a company's revenues, it's imperative for casino operators to discover who constitutes this one percent. Predictive analytics can monitor customer behavior and then build models that predict patron frequency and their individual worth into the future. This modeling can consolidate both gaming and non-gaming activity to show a patron's true property spend, an important distinction because it's not always the gambling patron who brings in the most revenue. At times of high demand, it's important for casino operators to know exactly how much a particular patron is worth so that they can fill the hotel only with their most profitable clients.

Up-sell and cross-sell

With predictive analytics, casino operators can enhance customer relationships by cross-selling and up-selling items that the customer might actually be interested in. Predictive analytics also enables call center personnel to act on inbound calls by providing offers that are likely to be attractive to certain caller profiles. Inversely, telemarketers can listen for such trigger phrases as "poker tournament" or "steak dinner" or "hotel room" to help casino marketers come up with the most enticing offer for the patron. In addition, automated systems like kiosks and customer service agents on the casino floor can use this predictive insight to provide customers with appropriate offers during other interactions.

Pearl River Resort: A Case Study

With 5,000 slot machines, 115 table games, 1,000 guest rooms, 14 restaurants, two golf courses, a water park, and a variety of shopping venues, Pearl River Resort is one of the largest casino resorts in the U.S. Known for its unsurpassed service, Pearl River Resort knew that understanding its guests was critical to meeting their needs. The goal at

Pearl River Resort was to figure out how to market to a casino property's current patrons as well as to increase the casino's overall market share. The predictive analytic solution that was implemented consolidated the casino's vast customer data into a clear picture of guest preferences. With this information, casino marketing executives were able to manage timely, personalized customer communication strategies that helped increase the casino resort's revenues.

For John Enriquez, Pearl River's former VP of Information Technology, guest knowledge was the fuel for resort marketing. The more thoroughly you know your guest, Enriquez believes, the more effective your marketing efforts will probably be. "Today's gaming enthusiast and family vacationers have many travel options. As those options for gaming entertainment continue to grow, it becomes who they are, where they're coming from, why they're here, and what their likes and dislikes are. That insight offers an incredible advantage," says Enriquez. "We make sure that the information we collect is analyzed and presented in the form of actionable business intelligence," adds Enriquez. "We develop models for testing assumptions. We monitor and measure the impact of marketing campaigns so they can be optimized on the fly, in real time. In other words, we make sure we're fishing where the fish are," he notes.

When Pearl River initiated a marketing campaign aimed at a narrow segment of players they were surprised at the results. "We assumed that this segment was highly profitable. But when we looked carefully at all the data, we saw that our assumptions had been wrong. So we refined the campaign, adjusting and optimizing it until we achieved the results we desired," says Enriquez. It became apparent that not all high-value guests were the same, some actually weren't very big gamblers but their spend in other parts of the resort more than made up for their disinterest in gambling. After all, at times when the casino is hosting poker or blackjack tournaments, when the tables will be filled, it might be preferable to have clients who have no intention of taking up space in the casino.

Pearl River Resort consolidated its vast visitor data into a clear picture of guest profiles and market segments, giving Enriquez and the other resort executives the ability to manage timely, personalized customer communication strategies. Data sources fed into the solution module included gaming transaction data, guest demographic data and point-of-sale data from non-gaming activities, including purchases at the resort's hotel, its golf course, its water park and its many restaurants. The Pearl River Rewards program, which offers a tiered system of discounts and perks for registered guests, is also used to collect visitor data.

"If you approach your marketing strategy from a guest knowledge perspective, you'll know precisely which of your guests love to play golf, which love to shop, which want an appointment at the spa, and which want to visit the water park," says Enriquez. "Before they even arrive, you can schedule them for a round of golf or a soothing massage. You can make their dinner reservations — and even make sure the right bottle of wine is properly chilled and waiting for them at the table," he adds. It is this kind of customer information and predictive analytics that makes it easier for Pearl River Resort to deliver a memorable and meaningful guest experience that will, hopefully, keep the guest coming back year after year after year.

Conclusion

As I mentioned at the beginning of this chapter, there is an old adage in marketing circles that says it is far more cost effective to keep a customer than to get a new one. This is truer today than ever before. The good news for casino operators is that they have more ways than ever to get a complete view of their patrons. For some casinos, as little as a five percent improvement in customer retention can lead to a fifty percent gain in profitability. For example, by using predictive analytics, Harrah's was able to identify a small group of customers who accounted for about 30% of their overall gamblers. These customers spent between $100 and $499 per trip but actually accounted for about 80% of the casino's revenue and nearly 100% of the casino's profits[4]. By implementing data mining and predictive analytics, casino operators can not only keep their high-value customers happier longer but they can also use these tools to take high-value customers away from their competitors. Predictive analytics can also pinpoint customers who are most likely to defect to the competition often with enough lead-time to allow casino employees to intervene.

---

[4] Lucky Numbers, Casino Chain Mines Data on Its Gamblers, And Strikes Pay Dirt, 'Secret Recipe' Lets Harrah's Target Its Low-Rollers At the Individual Level. A Free-Meal 'Intervention' by Christina Binkley. *The Wall Street Journal*, Thursday, May 4, 2000.

CHAPTER TWO

THE INDUSTRY'S CURRENT STANDARD

"There is a very easy way to return from a casino with a small fortune: go there with a large one."
~Jack Yelton

Overview

From property-wide property management systems to individual patron Radio-Frequency Identification (RFID) technology that is embedded in a poker chip, casino operators have embraced technology more than any other industry. Property management systems perform the important functions of gaming machine revenue tracking and analysis, ticket-in/ticket-out, player tracking, and more. In this chapter, I will discuss the many systems available to casino operators that allow them to not only keep track of a patron's gambling habits but also to follow a patron's complete resort spend.

Property Management System

In the hospitality industry a property management system (sometimes referred to as an enterprise system) is a computerized system used to manage guest bookings, online reservations, point-of-sale purchases, telephone charges as well as a whole host of other hotel amenities. The property management system can be used to gather information from each one of the hotel's systems to calculate the guest's bill and monitor stock and even staff performance. Hotel property management systems can interface with central reservation systems and revenue or yield management systems, as well as with front office, back office and point-of-sale systems.

The functionality of today's property management system extends far beyond room keys and guest bills. The property management system has the ability to "talk" to a casino system, track guest history with precision, and, most importantly, seamlessly interface with the reservation systems at both single- and multi-property hotels.

The results generated by these multi-functional property management systems have already proven their worth. Many casinos have reaped the benefits of a seamless interface between the reservations system and the property management system, including time savings and the ability to sell more room nights because of accurate availability data. Also, the new property management system enhances operations by allowing properties to work with fewer software systems, thereby increasing efficiency and reducing the hassles of partnering with a multitude of software and hardware vendors.

Point-of-Sales Systems (POS)

Hospitality Point-of-Sales Systems (POS) are computerized systems incorporating registers, computers and peripheral equipment. POS systems are used in supermarkets, restaurants, hotels, stadiums, and casinos, as well as almost any other type of retail establishment. Like other point-of-sales systems these systems keep track of sales, labor and payroll exepenses. They may be accessed remotely by restaurant corporate offices, troubleshooters, or other authorized parties.

Graphic User Interface (GUI) Requirements

There are two primary types of information delivery offered to the end user community, a web-based environment operating within the casino's Intranet system and a broader user-base and client-based application that provides in-depth functionality to assigned users.

The reporting and analysis needs at the casino can include a wide array of deliverables in several different formats, including:

- **Information Delivery Portal**: This provides a centralized web-based source for information delivery. This environment utilizes a single sign-on and can be tailored for an individual's reporting and analysis options based on their level of security authorization.
- **Interactive web**: This provides complete flexibility with the source information that is stored within the data warehouse and the targeted data marts[5]. It is a key source for several of the reporting deliverables and interaction with the underlying data sources utilized across the organization. It provides pre-defined report templates that can surface information to the end user. It also allows the user to modify and create his or her own reusable report templates that can be setup as tabular, graphical or any combination thereof that they might wish to utilize.

---

[5] A data mart is a subset of an organizational data store, usually oriented to a specific purpose or major data subject, that may be distributed to support business needs. *DMReview Magazine* Glossary. Data Management Review and SourceMedia, Inc. 2008.

- **Operational Reporting**: Custom reports might need to be created for the primary data sources. These reports can be tailored to the user's specific needs.

Agilysys

Recognized as one of the hospitality industry's premier property management software solutions, Agilysys' Lodging Management System® (LMS) solution automates every aspect of hotel operations – from reservations and credit card processing to accounting and housekeeping. The LMS solution also links customer's gaming accounts to hotel accounts and the system is built on a platform that runs around the clock.

Agilysys' Visual One is a reliable property management solution. Operating under Microsoft Windows NT with a Microsoft SQL Server database, the Visual One Hotel System takes advantage of the latest Microsoft products such as Word, Excel and even Microsoft Fax for sending reservation confirmations to guests. All of Visual One's data is available to the user, so they can create customized reports using, for example, Seagate's Crystal Report Writer.

Aristocrat

Aristocrat's Casino Management System is an advanced on-line accounting system that tracks gaming machine activity. Aristocrat's solutions offer the following:

- Revenue statistics by machine for coin-in, gross drop, jackpots, fills, net win, operator pay, adjusted net win, theoretical win, actual and variance hold percentages,

average coin-in per day, average win per day, and number of days on-line;
- Manual and electronic meters for coin-in and coin-out, coin drop, jackpots, hand-pay jackpots, and cash drop by currency denomination and period;
- The ability to view revenue statistics by sub-game in a multi-game;
- Drop-to-date, current, week, month, quarter, year, rolling two-year, and lifetime reporting periods;
- Fiscal or calendar year user-defined financial periods;
- Comprehensive record layout with a type code file, including denomination, cabinet, style, manufacturer, progressive calculations, reel and hopper types;
- Progressive jackpot accrual allocations;
- User-defined machine bank statistics;
- Enhanced machine move procedures including pre-scheduling moves and conversions;
- Ability to find a machine by location, OASIS ID, MAC address, slot master ID, bank ID, manufacturer, status, description, and type ID or machine number;
- Maintenance utilities, including error checking and revenue adjustment capabilities;
- Add, edit, or delete multi-games and associated sub-games to create new multi-games;
- Import hard count and soft count and ticket count information effortlessly (http://www.aristocrat.com.au/).

Bally

Bally Technologies, Inc., invented the first slot data system in 1976 and today offers a full complement of products to help casino operators retain and reward customers, manage and forecast their finances, reduce risk, spot trends, and increase their security. Bally's solutions include the following:

- **ACSC™**: More than just a customer database, it's a powerful Suite of IBM® "iSeries®"-based products designed to manage casino, slots, and hospitality data. ACSC's line of slot monitoring, marketing, casino accounting, and hotel functions blends seamlessly with lodging management systems and HIS®, the world's standard in hospitality management systems (http://ballytech.com/systems/cms.htm).
- **CMS/400™**: Provides a full range of customizable software products to manage virtually every aspect of the casino's functions, including player enrollment, player tracking and analysis, table-game management, cage and credit accounting, and redemptions (http://ballytech.com/systems/cms.htm).
- **CMP™**: Equips a casino operation with accounting functions, including financial audits, credit lines/markers, reconciliation, regulatory reporting and compliance; management of player ratings for slots, tables and other games; marketing functionality including patron loyalty programs, multi-property support, single player cards, player extracts, direct mail,

group and promotion tracking, and hotel integration (http://ballytech.com/systems/cms.htm).

- **MCC™**: A complete suite of casino management systems with its flagship product, Open Casino Manager™. MCC offers a comprehensive array of flexible systems products, including slot accounting, table-games management, player tracking, cashless wagering solutions, and customizable marketing modules (http://ballytech.com/systems/cms.htm).
- **TableView™**: An innovative table management solution that lets casino operators replace their existing manual rating process with the ease and simplicity of electronic automation (http://ballytech.com/systems/cms.htm).

IGT Advantage System

One of the leaders in the gaming industry, IGT offers the Advantage System, which incorporates the following solutions:

- **IGT Advantage Bonusing™**: Rewards players with spontaneous and unique loyalty driven bonuses (https://www.igt.com/).
- **Patron Management**: A powerful player account management system that cultivates loyalty and creates unique marketing programs tailored to those players (https://www.igt.com/).
- **EZ Pay® Ticketing**: The ticketing system that revolutionized the casino industry. It allows casino operators to attract new players, reward valuable

customers, and package their entertainment offerings (https://www.igt.com/).

- **Table iD™**: A comprehensive automated table games solution that eliminates manual tasks and more precisely allocates marketing and comp dollars (https://www.igt.com/).
- **Visual Slot Performance™**: Helps casino operators visually interpret the floor by using full-color maps, which makes historical and real-time data easy to understand (https://www.igt.com/).
- **Mobile Data Access™**: Makes mission-critical company data accessible anywhere an Internet connection is offered (https://www.igt.com/).
- **Cage & Table Accounting**: Automates every aspect of a casino operator's cage and table games operations (https://www.igt.com/).
- **Machine Accounting**: Gives casino operators accountability of all gaming transactions, as well as an accurate reconciliation of their casino's accounting for every shift (https://www.igt.com/).

Kronos

With products such as iSeries Gaming, iSeries Timekeeper, iSeries Leave, iSeries Scheduler, Workforce Acquisition and 4510 Touch ID Terminal, Kronos offers workplace management solutions that help with gaming, time and attendance, absence management, scheduling, talent management and biometric data collection.

Developed specifically for the casino and gaming industry, the Kronos for Gaming solutions ensure that user's employees are paid properly and casino properties remain in compliance with federal and state labor related regulations. Kronos for Gaming allows users to cost-effectively enhance the customer experience by selecting, acquiring, and scheduling the right workforce to meet customer demand.

Micros OPERA

Powered by Oracle™, the Micros OPERA Enterprise Solution offers casino operators the ability to share information across multiple applications and properties on a single database while providing the necessary enterprise software solutions and tools for Property and Central operations. The OPERA Property Management System handles reservations, guest check-in and check-out, room assignment and managing room inventory, as well as accommodating in-house guest needs, and handling accounting and billing functions. The application is configurable to each property's specific requirements and operates in either single-property or multi-property mode, with all properties in a complex sharing a single database.

SpaSoft

An industry-standard for more than 10 years, SpaSoft combines advanced technological prowess with sound operational knowledge. The end result is a user-friendly, robust application designed to assist in the total management of any spa.

Conclusion

Today's casino operators have a multitude of software solutions to chose from and the options are almost overwhelming. Property management systems from vendors such as Agilysys, Kronos, and Micros must function seamlessly with gaming systems from Ballys or IGT, while working on multiple databases and operating systems that could be using a variety of software systems, such as Teradata, Oracle, Sybase, DB2 and SQL/Server. It's enough to give any IT manager a migraine.

CHAPTER THREE

CASINO MARKETING

"However beautiful the strategy, you should occasionally look at the results."
~Winston Churchill

Overview

Often referred to as the heartbeat of casino operations, marketing effects almost every single function in a modern casino property yet it is often taken for granted. Casino marketing involves not only providing the right offer to the right patron at the right time, but it also includes retaining existing patrons as well as acquiring new ones. To perform these tasks, the casino marketer needs to not only fully understand the patrons in its database but also figure out how to get new patrons onto its property and into its databases. To allocate resources properly as well as to attract and retain the most profitable customer segments, the casino marketing department needs to understand which segments "pay the bills." Some of the questions they must ask are:

- Who are the casino's current customers?
- Which customer segments contribute the most or the least to the property's revenue?
- Does it make more sense to design promotions that attract player segments with low theoretical win levels but high frequency of visitation or should the casino allocate promotional dollars to player segments with higher theoretical win rates but less frequent visitations?

- Where do the casino's customers live?
- What is the overall contribution of each zip code?

All of this information is critical when a casino decides how to allocate its advertising dollars. In general, the casino marketing department must decide if it makes more sense to continue to maintain a strong presence in traditional feeder markets or if the casino should target new ones.

Market Segmentation

In their article *How a professional casino consultant can help 'optimize' your casino's marketing*, Steve Karoul and Dean Macomber advise casino marketers to think of their potential market as a series of interconnecting circles of differing categories within which there is an endless variety of options. They state that the segments can include, but are not limited to, the following:

1. Geographic
2. Demographic
3. Psychological
4. Cultural
5. Age
6. Activities

When broken down this way, one person would obviously be included in many different categories. Each segment would be broken down into smaller segments. For geography, there would be three segments — Nearby or "convenience" gaming customers, to whom distance matters a lot; Middle distances or "excursion" gaming customers, to whom distance is somewhat of an issue; and Large distances or the "destination" gaming customers, to whom distance matters little (Karoul and Macomber).

Demographically, casino operators can look at the age, occupation, social class, income level, and marital status of their customers (Karoul and Macomber).

In the psychological category, casino operators can look at whether the customer would be considered a ring leader, i.e., is he or she the person who draws a lot of other people in or, to put it more simply, is he or she the one responsible for organizing the bachelor or bachelorette party that brought in an additional ten guests? Details such as whether this customer is a social-monger, a risk-taker or a sports fan can also be included here (Karoul and Macomber).

Cultural and ethnicity is a very important segment to know because certain ethnicities are more prone to gambling than others (Karoul and Macomber). Gambling is ingrained within the Asian cultures more so than any other culture in the world, whereas in Middle Eastern cultures gambling is a sin according to the Koran.

Age is an important segment in understanding the customer's lifetime value to the property. Segments would include such things as whether the customer has recently turned twenty-one and can start gambling, whether they are in their thirties or forties, a time when they would have more disposable income but possibly less time available for gambling. A final segment would be senior citizens, a time in life when customers might be interested in slot tournaments and a time when extra effort must be put into getting the customer to the casino, as they may not have easy access to transportation.

Activities could include the customer's interest in such resort offerings as golf, tennis, or spa activities, or any other specific recreation, including shows, boxing matches, concerts, special events, entertainment, shopping, etc., (Karoul and Macomber).

With market segmentation, casino operators can identify a specific property or marketing objective and promote the property 'outwards.' For example, if a property wants to increase revenue at its blackjack tables during a slow midweek period, they can identify blackjack players who have either shown up to play in midweek before or who have the propensity to do so. Once these players are identified, a casino marketing program can tailor laser-focused marketing campaigns to these individuals. As with all other marketing campaigns they should tap into the customer's needs, wants and expectations (Karoul and Macomber).

Marketing Cycle and Demand Creation

When creating their marketing strategies, casino operators must think in terms of the Market Cycle of Demand Creation, which contains the following three phases:

1. Awareness
2. Trial offer
3. Repeated visitation (Karoul and Macomber).

Consumers must first know that the product — the casino — exists. When a casino opens, it must create awareness about itself, whether that is through standard advertising venues such as television, radio and print. First, the casino marketer must motivate people to come to the casino. Once patrons are there, casino marketers must then turn first-time visitors into loyal customers who will repeatedly return. Casino operators can do this by offering their first-time patrons incentives to enroll in the casino's player card program. Once enrolled, the casino marketers can track the player's spend, determine their likes and dislikes and then target market to them. At this point, casino marketers will develop a range of programs and offers that should generate repeated visits (Karoul and Macomber).

Marketing Campaigns

This is where the rubber meets the road. Some of the standard current casino marketing campaigns include:

- **Monthly Direct Mail**: Offers are provided to patrons in a monthly mailing. This usually consists of several offers for room, food or cash/credits that are redeemable during the month. Offer values are usually based upon the patron's theoretical win ratio.
- **Birthday**: Monthly campaigns for patrons whose birthdays occur during the concurrent month.
- **Promotions**: Campaigns that may contain invitations to events like slot or poker tournaments, concerts or other special events.

Automating and Streamlining the Campaign Processes

A marketing automation tool will provide a user-friendly mechanism for assigning the data specific requirements to identify the segments. Once the marketing campaign criterion is established, all future campaigns can be assured of having the same criteria. This type of tool will then provide a simple point and click method for breaking each of the segments into smaller, more targeted cells. These cells can then be associated with specific coupon codes, based on both the cell and the dates that the communications are issued. It is also at this point that the criteria for determining if a customer responded are established. When coupons are redeemed, it is then a simple matter of linking the coupon codes to the original communication codes. The main advantage of an automation tool is that every campaign, communication, cell and response can be attributed to a specific event. All of this is achievable because every step is automatically coded and stored. The tool then ensures that no codes are erroneously reused, while at the same time providing a common interface to include, exclude or reuse customers involved in prior communications

Scheduling campaigns will allow the team to set-up recurring campaigns weeks in advance versus setting up individual campaigns one at a time. The goal is to automate routine processes into regularly scheduled jobs. These jobs will have various scheduling options that will allow for time and/or processing dependency triggers (e.g. offer redemption or non-response). This will eliminate the need for manual program processing and data manipulation.

Predictive Modeling

Predictive modeling is only useful if it is deployed *and* it creates an action. There needs to be an easy way to incorporate valid models into the selection process. The results should be available in simple reports that are comprehensible and easy for the marketers to understand.

Taking advantage of the more powerful, statistically based segmentation methods, customers can be segmented not only on dollar values, but also on all known information, which can include behavioral information gleaned from resort activities as well as the patron's simple demographic information. This more detailed segmentation allows for more targeted and customer-focused marketing campaigns.

Models can be evaluated and reports generated on multiple statistical measures, such as lift and gains charts[6]. Once built, scores can be generated in a variety of ways to facilitate quick and easy implementation. The projects themselves can be re-used and shared to facilitate faster model development and knowledge transfer.

By utilizing data from past campaigns and measures generated by the predictive modeling process, casino operators can track actual campaign responses versus expected campaign responses, which can often diverge wildly. Additionally, casino operators can generate upper and lower "control" limits that can be used to automatically alert campaign managers when a campaign is over or underperforming, therefore they can focus on campaigns that specifically need their attention.

One of the benefits of automating campaigns is that offers can be developed that are based on either stated or inferred preferences of patrons. Analysis can identify which customers may be more responsive to a food/beverage offer, a room offer, and/or a free tournament offer. This results in making offers more relevant to individual patrons and therefore increases campaign success by, once again, tapping into the customer's needs, wants and expectations.

Campaign Effectiveness: Capturing Response Data

To truly understand the success or failure of a marketing campaign, casino operators must have an effective response tracking system. Costs and revenues can be combined with promotional contact and response

---

[6] Cumulative gains and lift charts are visual aids for measuring model performance.

information, which will provide a complete picture of response rates and ROI. Because this information is stored at the individual customer level, various levels of modeling, segmentation and analysis can be performed for strategic targeting of a campaign.

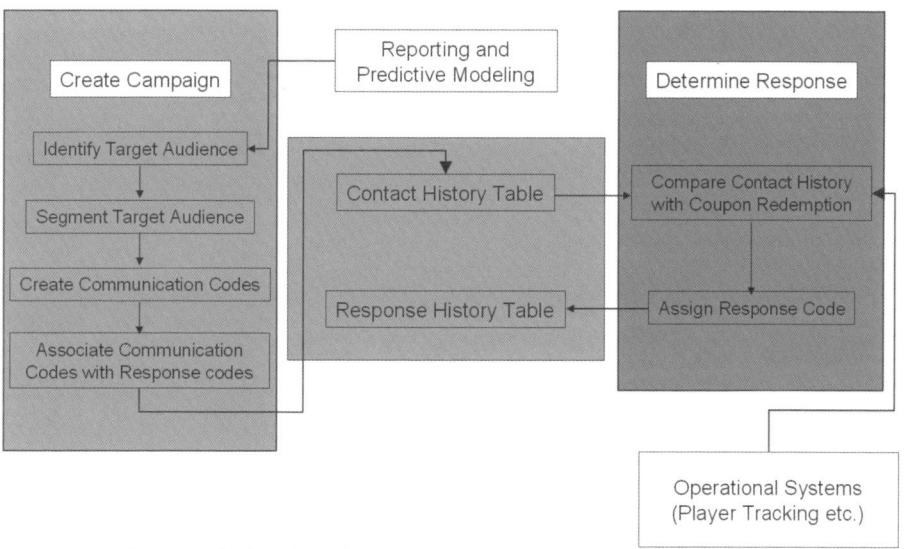

Figure 3.1: Example of a campaign illustrating desired capabilities.

Social Networking and Microblogs: Valuable Unfiltered Information

With the rise of social networks and online communities such as Facebook, MySpace, Yelp and Twitter, which provide instantaneous and unfiltered information, casino marketers can now upgrade their CRM programs to interact with their customers on a highly personal level. This is access that is invaluable as casino marketers can now reach previous guest and upcoming visitors and engage them in new and important ways. Casino marketers can identify past guests by searching through Facebook or

MySpace and tag members who mention "Vegas" in their profiles. Once these individuals are identified, casino marketers can target them with specific offers, i.e., if someone mentions they like to play blackjack, the marketer can send emails with $25 coupons that can be redeemed on the customer's next visit.

Casino operators can cultivate a powerful two-way relationship with their customers online by developing microblogs that encourage users to follow a corporate persona via Twitter. These blogs can either be informative or they can offer promotional content. Most importantly, they open a two-way conversation with the casino consumer.

Conclusion

At the beginning of this chapter, I mentioned that casino marketing has often been referred to as the heartbeat of casino operations and, just like a heart, casino marketing can never stop. In the current business climate, it is imperative to create a long lasting brand relationship between patron and casino property. Casino marketers can do this by understanding their patron's needs, wants and expectations and then marketing directly to those needs, wants and expectations.

Casino operators should not be reluctant to dive into social media options because of their unfiltered nature. These forums will exist with or without the involvement of casino operators, therefore it's better to get ahead of the curve rather than be stuck behind it.

A marketing automation solution can help a casino operator improve response rates and raise revenues by giving it the ability to easily manage sophisticated, timely, personalized customer communication strategies.

I have not mentioned mobile marketing, which is the latest cutting-edge marketing technology available to casino operators because I believe this topic deserves a chapter of its own and that is the subject of the next chapter.

CHAPTER FOUR

MOBILE-IZE YOUR MARKETING: THE VIRAL IMPACT

"Selling to people who actually want to hear from you is more effective than interrupting strangers who don't."
~Seth Godin

"But isn't it all a bit intrusive?"
~Anonymous digital agency chief[7]

Overview

2008 will probably be known as the year that marked the end of the beginning for mobile web technology. Currently, there are over three billion cell phone users in the world. The cell phone has become the ubiquitous "third screen" for most people. Only a few short years ago, U.S. mobile users were embracing color screens, now they can watch full video on their phones. The U.S. market is actually way behind the European and Asian markets, which embraced Short Message Service (SMS)[8] technology years ago. Today's mobile phones, specifically the iPhone 3G, the Blackberry Storm, and the G1 Android have screens large enough to display a lot of information on.

Initially, mobile marketing via SMS was viewed as a new type of spam but, under the watchful eye of the Mobile Marketing Association, guidances were put in place to reduce spam and now in Europe over 100 million SMS advertisements are sent out each month. One of the key criteria is that consumers opt in to the service. Mobile marketing is

---

[7] http://www.mobilemarketingmagazine.co.uk/2006/07/wakeup_call.html (accessed March 1, 2009)
[8] Short Message Service (SMS) is a communication service standardized in the GSM mobile communication system, using standardized communications protocols allowing the interchange of short text messages between mobile telephone devices

primarily a "pull" media model, meaning a consumer must sign up for the service rather than the traditional "push" media model, which gives the consumer no choice in whether they want to be advertised to or not. Mobile marketers must spend money to get users to sign up, but if they do, the potential market for mobile marketing is huge and rapidly evolving. Its advantages include:

- Ubiquity - cell phone users and their cell phones are everywhere
- Over 90% of text messages are read by the recipient
- Instantaneous link between business and customer
- Economical
- Spam-free

Mobile users are increasingly using SMS technology to access information about brands and products they find interesting. SMS was developed to provide companies with an easier, more creative and cost effective way to reach their customers and many companies have embraced the technology in some very imaginative ways, including:

- The NBA and NFL allow their fans to vote for their all stars with SMS.
- Major League Baseball (MLB) alerts fans with MLB-related offers.
- Pizza Hut allows their customers to order pizzas through their cell phones.
- Wendy's lets potential employees send an SMS text to hear about employment opportunities.

- The Obama campaign announced their vice presidential pick via an SMS text.
- The Boston police use SMS for crime tip reporting.
- Verizon uses SMS to deliver Yellow Pages information.
- Fandango uses SMS to link users to movie information by zip code.
- ABC, CBS, Fox, NBC and Bravo use SMS for interactive voting.
- Google uses SMS for search results.
- Hooters made their calendar girls available for mobile download.
- Harlequin offers free romance novels to iPhone users.
- The British soccer club Aston Villa turned to SMS to fill seats.
- Google will be making over 1.5 million public domain books available to iPhones and Android-enabled devices.
- J.C. Penney allowed users to sign up for a wakeup call so they wouldn't miss a Black Friday sale.

Mobile consumers are primed to accept SMS marketing if it is used in an interesting and creative way. For example, in November 2008, Casino giant Harrah's ran a mobile couponing pilot program as part of its customer loyalty program. Working with a mobile marketing service provider, Harrah's sent out time-based and location-based offers in real time to the mobile devices of their Total Rewards customers. Offers included free parking, free cocktails and free in-venue entertainment. The codes were customized to be used once, or several times, or they were even coded in a way that allowed recipients to forward them virally. The mobile program, branded T.I.P. for Texting Important People, was tested at three of Harrah's properties — Harrah's Atlantic City, Harrah's New Orleans and Showboat Atlantic City — and proved quite successful[9].

Harrah's has embraced mobile technology, even allowing customers to join their Total Rewards loyalty program by texting the keyword 'Harrah's' to a five-digit code. Sign up is instantaneous and customers immediately receive mobile coupons via text messages that are then redeemable at one of Harrah's properties[10].

Mobile Marketing: Endless Options

Mobile marketing is unique in that a customer must opt in to the marketing to get started. Once they have, however, company marketers have a direct one-on-one connection with their customer. An SMS shortcode can be added to:

- Radio advertisements
- Newspaper and magazine advertisements
- Billboards
- Product packaging
- Corporate literature and flyers
- Event invitations
- Websites

---

[9] http://www.dmnews.com/Harrahs-makes-loyalty-mobile/article/121543/ (Accessed March 1, 2009).
[10] http://www.mobilemarketer.com/cms/news/database-crm/2137.html (Accessed March 1, 2009).

When it comes to mobile marketing, casino marketers are limited only by their imagination, but however they wish to proceed their mobile marketing campaigns should include the following:

- **Mobile Coupons**: These are text messages that include coupon codes that can be used by the casino patrons in the resort's restaurants, bars, salons, spas or any another establishment on the property where management wants to enhance business. The patrons simply show the code when paying their bill. Mobile coupon ideas are limitless and can be very creative, including:

  - Free $25 chip for play at a particular table
  - 20% coupon for the casino's restaurant
  - Buy one drink, get a second drink free coupon for a casino bar
  - Free two-night stay on the customer's next trip to the casino
  - "No cover" entry for patrons who are standing in line to get into one of the casino's exclusive nightclubs
  - $25 off the price of a wedding ceremony
  - 10% off a spa service
  - $20 off a round of golf

- **Wap Push:** A WAP Push is a specially encoded message that includes a hyperlink to an Internet address. This could be the site where a new customer can sign up for a player reward card or just a web page that includes information about the goings-on in the casino or on the property.

- **Txt2Win:** One of the best ways to collect mobile phone numbers is to hold a contest in which participants have to text a code from their mobile phone. The casino simply has to put up signage about the competition and it can then decide exactly how many customers have to be enrolled before a winner is announced.
- **SMS Blast:** Messages can be sent quickly and easily to anyone on the casino's marketing list. Within seconds, a customer can receive a message about restaurant offers, availability at a poker table, the current jackpot on their favorite slot machine, or a whole host of other messages that the casino chooses to include.
- **Click to Call**: Messages can contain a clickable link on a mobile web page that triggers a phone call.
- **Educational Downloads:** Gamblers who want to learn about a particular casino game can request information via a text message. Videos that explain gambling games can be sent directly to the mobile users phone.

Picture Messaging and Bar Codes

For mobile marketers the future is already here. Nike 6.0, the footwear giant's action sports brand, recently ran a mobile 2D bar code campaign targeting teens at the Winter Dew Tour[11], At every Dew Tour event,

---

[11] The Winter Dew Tour is an action sports tour sponsored by Mountain Dew

pictures of athletes that contained 2D bar codes were posted. If consumers took a photograph of these barcodes with their cell phones and then sent the picture message to a certain short code, they received a short video clip featuring that athlete. Because the 2D bar code works on every camera phone on the Verizon Wireless and AT&T network without any additional applications, consumers were easily able to utilize this feature. This gives marketers the ability to deliver audio, video and pictures to a mass mobile audience[12]. If a casino wants to educate players on how to play one of their casino games, mobile users can have short video lessons sent to their mobile phones. Advertisements for casino shows, gambling events or sporting activities can also be sent directly to the casino patron's mobile phones.

Mobile Loyalty

At the Rio All Suite Hotel and Casino in Las Vegas, Harrah's uses mobile marketing to target personalized promotions to opted-in users. The company provides real time offers, property information and Total Rewards Club loyalty points balance to Rio guests on their mobile phones[13]. With perishable inventory such as show or concert tickets or restaurant seats, mobile marketing can send out instant discount codes to opted-in customers. The discount codes are redeemable for vouchers at any Total Rewards booth. This way, a ten-dollar offer coupon could entice patrons to visit a show and purchase seats that would otherwise have gone unfilled. The challenge then is to predict which perishable items are going

---

[12] http://www.mobilemarketer.com/cms/news/messaging/2629.html (Accessed March 1, 2009).
[13] http://www.casinocitytimes.com/news/article.cfm?contentID=177056 (Accessed March 1, 2009).

to go unused and then to figure out how to connect to the customer most likely to be interested in the offer. After all, most men probably wouldn't be too interested in receiving the $10 Chippendales ticket offer Rio often sends out to promote that particular show.

Mobile Analytics

Mobile analytics — the use of data collected as visitors access a web site from a mobile phone — can effectively track unique visitors, as well as the visitor's country, network and device responding to a mobile ad campaign. With site analysis added to a mobile analytics service, casino operators can capture mobile metrics such as link tracking for campaign analysis and page tracking for site analysis.

Data collected as part of mobile analytics typically includes information such as page views, visits, and visitors and also such mobile specific information as: mobile device, mobile network operator or carrier, country, language and a unique user ID, which is required because http cookies and JavaScript do not work reliably on mobile browsers. This data is typically compared against key performance indicators for performance and return on investment, and is used to improve a web site or mobile marketing campaign's audience response.

Collecting mobile web analytics data is not as simple as traditional web analytics because many of the common methods for data collection do not work and can provide misleading data that actually under reports mobile traffic.

Conclusion

Mobile marketing is so powerful and unique because it is an interactive, always-on, cross-media channel that allows consumers to instantly move from the ad placement to a point-of-sale site, whether that site is an online store, a casino floor, or a restaurant or bar. Mobile marketing is here to stay and will probably change mobile consumer shopping habits the way the Internet changed retail consumer habits. Basically, anything that can make the life of your customer easier and more efficient is a good option for a mobile marketing campaign. The options and potential of this new marketing strategy are truly endless and must be embraced by all casino operators.

CHAPTER FIVE

RADIO FREQUENCY IDENTIFICATION

"The guy who invented poker was bright, but the guy who invented the chip was a genius."
~Author unknown

Overview

Radio Frequency Identification (RFID) was originally conceived in 1948 and the technology has taken a slow road to acceptance since it evolved from such systems as the long range transponder system of IFF (Identification Friend or Foe), which came out of the radar and radio research undertaken during the Second World War. Widely used in the retail sector, RFID is now gaining acceptance in the casino industry because of the inherent advantages it has over bar code technology.

RFID is a rapidly growing technology. According to Gaming Partners International, one of the leading RFID technology companies, RFID chips accounted for 3.4% of their sales in 2004, 12.7% in 2005, 35% in 2006, and 26.7% in 2007. Progressive Gaming's RFID systems have been deployed in over 25 casinos in North America. Internationally, they have been installed in several Macau casinos, including Wynn Macau, Crown Macau and the Galaxy StarWorld Casino. RFID chips are here to stay because they give casino operators the power to not only monitor the behavior of gamblers but also the ability to spot counterfeits and thefts.

How It Works

RFID tags are devices that can be inserted into a product, an animal, or even a person[14] so that they can be identified using radio waves. Most RFID tags contain both an integrated circuit for storing and processing information, modulating and demodulating a signal and an antenna for receiving and transmitting the signal. RFID technology has six primary advantages over bar code technology and they are:

1. **Uniqueness**: RFID tags have their own unique code, which allows them to be accounted for individually;
2. **Concealment:** RFID tags can be hidden inside a casino chip, which can then be scanned in such a way that the individual holding it is unaware f the scanning;
3. **Speed:** RFID allows for nearly instantaneous reading of multiple chips;
4. **Storage capacity:** RFID tags can hold considerably more information than bar codes;
5. **Two-way communication ability:** RFID tags can communicate to an outside PC and vice-versa;
6. **Modifiability**: RFID tags can be updated constantly with new and important information (Wyld, 2005).

---

[14] http://www.globalresearch.ca/index.php?context=va&aid=10097 (Accessed March 1, 2009).

In terms of the house advantage, slot machines are the king of casino games but table games draw more high rollers and these are the customers casino operators prefer to see in their casinos. High rollers bet the most and therefore lose the most, which, in turn, means they are the most eligible for comps and perks. Today, with RFID technology casinos have the ability to keep track of every dollar their high rollers spend and this can go a long way to ensure that high roller comps are doled out equitably. Currently, in an effort to err on the side of caution, it is estimated that casino operators are overshooting their comps and perks by about 20 to 30 percent (Gilbert, 2005). RFID's great advantage is its ability to identify individual players and associate them with a particular tag or chip.

Currently, companies such as Gaming Partners International, CHIPCO International, and Progressive Gaming offer playing chips that are embedded with RFID chips as well as the gaming tables that these chips are to be played on. These tables are equipped with a PC that can read up to seven betting stations that hold up to twenty chips at each seat in less than a second. This speed will soon be eclipsed by a new generation of gaming tables. The accuracy in which these chips can be read means the casino can instantaneously know how much a particular patron starts the session with, how much his or her average bet is, what his preferred method of play is, even how generous a tipper he is. Knowing this precise information, the pit boss can offer comps to the player that accurately reflects his or her patron value.

Tracking of the gaming chips doesn't end on the casino floor. Playing chips can be tracked from the cage, to the vault, to chip banks, to tables and to chip trays. This gives the casino real time monitoring of chip inventory, instant chip validation at the cage and even provides the movement history of each chip during the course of its lifetime, thereby reducing the casino's vulnerability to chip theft or counterfeiting. Overall, this technology allows casino operators to:

- Initiate player ratings
- Perform table accounting functions
- Input head count and drop information
- View instant spread analyses of the floor
- Spot player behavior that could reveal card counting
- Uncover dealer mistakes or dealer cheating
- See real time data on individual players as well as their dealers
- Give exact player tipping information

Monitoring Play

Casinos spend millions of dollars every year in an effort to catch cheaters and card counters. The casino's 'eye-in-the-sky' cameras record every roll of the dice, every flip of the card and every spin of the roulette wheel. RFID-based table-monitoring systems can help casino operators not only keep track of their customers but also keep tabs on their employees. With RFID-enabled table-monitoring systems, dealers can easily catch gamblers who try to sneak chips on or off the table during a game, a process know as "pastposting" (Sturgeon, 2005).

Card Counters: Count Them out

It's quite ironic that the technology that evolved out of a long-range transponder system that was used to identify friend from foe in the World

War Two skies over England is now being used to uncover one of the casino industry's most dangerous foes — the card counter. With RFID technology, the card counter could be revealed when he or she uses the card counter's specific accelerated betting strategy when he or she notices a certain pattern of dealt cards. The more low cards dealt early in the shoe means that more high cards exist in the remaining decks. Since more high cards in the deck tilt the advantage to the player (because statistically the house is more likely to go bust in this scenario), card counters then tend to bet more heavily. Although not too difficult to spot, these strategies require a lot of personnel time to uncover. With RFID-embedded chips, a casino can track a patron's exact gambling strategy and this strategy can be instantaneously cross-referenced with a program that is specifically design to reveal card counting. Compared to similar human observation methods, which might require the time of several human beings, from pit bosses to surveillance agents, this method would be much faster, which could mean substantial savings in employee time. Human error is also removed. Armed with this irrefutable evidence, casino management can then intervene and banish the individual from the casino (Wyld, 2008).

Casino operators need to be more vigilant than ever before because card-counting technology is only going to get more and more sophisticated. Recently, Nevada State Gaming Control officials warned casinos about a new iPhone application that can simplify card counting. Used in stealth mode, the program allows a user to simply tap one virtual button for any card 10 or higher and another virtual button for any card 9 or lower. The software program will continuously update the "true count,"[15] which would be of considerable help to card counters.

---

[15] http://tech.yahoo.com/news/afp/20090216/tc_afp/usitinternetgamblingtelecomapple (Accessed March 1, 2009)

Theft and Counterfeit

With RFID technology embedded inside a chip, casino operators can be almost absolutely certain about the authenticity of their chips. Casinos wouldn't have to rely on the dealers, cashiers, and supervisors to verify the genuineness of a casino chip. Currently, the only backups casinos have are special inks that casinos routinely use to mark their chips — marks that can only be viewed in infrared or ultraviolet light. With these imperfect controls, many industrious thieves have attempted to create counterfeit chips. For example, in April, 2005, two men were arrested for minting and cashing $50,000 worth of casino chips at several casinos in southern Nevada. With the help of a computer scanner, an airbrush, paint, glitter and an industrial blow dryer, the accused had turned $1 casino chips into $100 casino chips[16]. These men turned a $1 investment into a $99 profit. If only we could all see such returns.

    Since each RFID chip would be assigned to specific individuals, the identify of the chip would be known so if these chips ended up in the pocket of anyone but it's rightful owner, the casino would have irrefutable evidence that it had been stolen, either internally or by another customer. Currently, when a casino can't find a large stash of chips, it is forced to not only change its entire stock of chips but also force gamblers to exchange their old chips for new ones, which obviously can be a very difficult endeavor, and it can infuriate the casino's gamblers. Going forward, the old chips would be considered worthless, which means some gamblers could potentially lose the entire value of those chips if they didn't exchange them in time. RFID chips wouldn't face this problem as chips

---

[16] http://www.majorwager.com/forums/mess-hall/37716-two-charged-counterfeiting-casino-chips-nevada.html (Accessed March 1, 2009)

can now be associated with both a player and a table and, once the chip leaves its assigned area, casino security could be alerted.

Responsible Gaming

Unfortunately, problem gamblers are a part of the casino industry and it is the responsibility of casino operators to identify them and assist them in getting help for their addiction. Although not the most common addiction, gambling addiction has the highest suicide rate of any addition[17]. Currently, casinos train their employees to spot compulsive gamblers but that is not always an easy thing to do. Addictive gamblers don't stand out the way alcoholics do. They are often educated, married and have children so casino employees must look for subtle behavioral clues. It's not as simple as keeping an eye out for the customer who repeatedly heads to the ATM to get more money to feed his or her addiction. Casino employees have to look for gamblers who linger at the same machine or table for hours on end and show little emotion when they win big, which is not exactly uncommon behavior on a casino floor. While not completely replacing human observation, RFID-enhanced tracking of table game play can give casino operators better player intelligence so that they can intervene at appropriate times. After all, casino operators want their patron's recreational dollars, not their life savings.

Beyond Chips: A Different Smart Card

Several companies are now developing playing cards that have RFID technology embedded within them. By associating players with cards,

---

[17] http://www.nctimes.com/articles/2007/04/04/news/state/030307152252.prt (Accessed March 1, 2009)

casinos will also be able to track a player's strategy, which should reveal if they are card counters or they just happen to be on a lucky streak (Wyld, 2008). RFID will also let casinos track cards and chips in a poker game, which could be useful for security purposes as well as adding a new element to the game by letting online players participate in poker games that are being played in distant casino (Wyld, 2008). Current Internet gambling laws might not allow this but, as I discuss later in the book, legislation has been proposed to allow poker playing on the Internet.

Conclusion

The potential inherent in RFID technology is enormous. Besides the time savings this technology offers, casino operators can create a very accurate picture of a player's gambling habits. Throughout the life cycle of the player, casino operators can measure their average bets, their tips and their game choices. Casino operators can also track a player's every move throughout the casino. If a player starts at a blackjack table and then moves to the sports book, where he tips a waitress with an RFID chip, the casino can know roughly how much time he spends in there. Most importantly, RFID technology lets casino operators take the guess work out of doling out comps to their players as well as track their player's gambling strategies to spot cheats.

CHAPTER SIX

TABLE-GAMES REVENUE MANAGEMENT

"If you are not taking care of your customer, your competitor will."

~Bob Hooey

Overview

Revenue management, also know as yield management, is the process of maximizing revenue and profits from a perishable resource by understanding, anticipating and, most importantly, influencing customer behavior. First discovered by Dr. Matt H. Keller, the challenge with revenue management is to figure out how to sell the right resource to the right customer at the right time for the right price (Yeoman and Ingold, 1997). Such diverse companies as American Airlines, NBC, GM and UPS have successfully implemented revenue management and casino operators can also apply revenue management techniques to table games management. In some ways, they already do. When a casino pit boss manipulates table minimum wagers to either entice more volume or to select the most financially attractive players, he is basically using a rudimentary form of revenue management (Krigman, 1995). The revenue management tools available to casino operators today should banish this very unscientific revenue management method to ancient Las Vegas history, right alongside the El Rancho, the Desert Inn, the Aladdin, the Dunes, and all of the other imploded palaces of yesterday.

In this chapter, I will specifically discuss the subject of table-games revenue management because this is an area that is currently being under-utilized by casino operators and lends itself perfectly to exploitation by predictive analytics. By applying survival analysis[18] to revenue management models, casino operators can gain a truer picture of table games revenue (Peister, 2007). When a casino operator adds another layer of analysis — predictive analytics of the individual players at the table — onto those models, they can get a very accurate picture of capacity and supply and thereby manipulate table minimums with a confidence they have never had before.

Table-Games Revenue Management (TGRM): Demand Based Pricing

As mentioned above, revenue management tries to sell the right product to the right customer for the right price at the right time, but in order to do this the following conditions must be in place:

- Supply is relatively fixed
- The product is perishable
- The creation of a new supply is prohibitive

With a fixed supply and a highly perishable product, table games are subject to the classic revenue management constraints (Peister, 2007). Table games minimums are manipulated by pit bosses according to need, and, in this regard, they differ from machine games. Seats at a table are an extremely perishable product. Whereas hotels can't realistically sell rooms for less than a twenty-four-hour period, table games have hundreds of possible permutations, including from having as little as one person

---

[18] Survival analysis attempts to answer questions such as: what is the fraction of a population which will survive past a certain time? Of those that survive, at what rate will they die or fail? Can multiple causes of death or failure be taken into account? How do particular circumstances or characteristics increase or decrease the odds of survival? (www.wikipedia.com)

playing at a table to having as many as seven people there, and these people can gamble anywhere in the range of a minimum of $1 to a maximum bet of over $250 and just about anything in between, if so desired (Peister, 2007). The factors that can be manipulated are the number of hands played and the average bet played. The objective of table-games revenue management is to manage the relationship between hands played and average bet (Peister, 2007). According to Peister:

> "Time is best characterized by available seating hours, a measurement that captures capacity and is not skewed by player or dealer skill levels or by table occupancy (which would be the case with measuring available hands, for example). The complete metric is stated as win per available seating hour or WPASH. WPASH is calculated by dividing win by available seating hours (where available seating hours is the number of usable seats x hours in the time interval)."

The problem for casino operators is the fact that a revenue manager might fail to take into account the unrealized players who are waiting for a table seat to open up and then underestimate true demand and thereby offer too many low minimum tables and too few premium tables. This effect, known as a negative bias, can be very costly to the casino's bottom line. Studying negative bias in the airline industry, Lawrence Weatherford discovered that understating demand by 12.5 percent could lead to a 0.7 to 1.2 percent decrease in revenues (Zeni, 2001).

The fundamental goal of any revenue management system is to maximize revenue per unit whereas the goal of a table-games revenue management scheme is to manage the relationship between hands played and average bet (Peister, 2007). "Unlike hotels, however, there is not the opportunity to double-book a seat, and thus the maximum possible number of hands is 100 percent of hands offered. From a revenue management perspective, the goal is to maximize WPASH even if that entails available table time perishing as unoccupied," Peister adds. The second problem in this equation is the inability to truly measure demand, as would-be players will only linger around busy tables for so long. Even if there were a way to count these people, it would almost be impossible to figure out at what minimum bets they would prefer to play. Although logic suggests that table games revenue can easily be increased by manipulating minimum wagers, the matter is complicated by the nature of games, which allow "partial sales," (i.e., any number of hands) but do not allow a bet of zero, and in which actual demand is censored (when people are waiting to play).

Now, however, casino operators are on the threshold of having a truly predictive table-games revenue management system available to them. The information that casino operators need to predict how long a seat might remain filled is available from an individual's player card data as well as the data casino operators can glean from these player's RFID chips. When a patron sits down at a table, the casino can run predictive analytics that take into account how much he buys in for, how much he historically tends to wager on each hand, whether he tends to re-buy in or not, and what the house's inherent advantage on the type of game he is playing. The results of this computation should tell the casino how long they can expect the patron to gamble for and, therefore, how long he or she will fill up the table seat. The data can be constantly updated as one player could hit a hot streak or be pulled away from the table for one reason or another. These predictive analytics could be invaluable information for the casino and it would help pit bosses figure out how best to manipulate table minimums and thereby maximize revenue. Most of the information that is needed is already contained within the casino's databases so there is little need for expensive hardware and software purchases to implement this system.

Conclusion

There is no reason why a revenue management model can't be applied to other areas of a casino as well as to the property management system. Anywhere a casino needs to fill seats, they can apply a revenue management model to it. For example, if a revenue management model was coupled with mobile analytics, casino operators could instantly connect with their patrons and send them offers that could fills seats at a show or in a restaurant that would otherwise have gone unused.

CHAPTER SEVEN

THE CASINO FLOOR: A BRAVE NEW WORLD

"Remember this: The house doesn't beat the player. It just gives him the opportunity to beat himself."
~Nicholas (Nick the Greek) Dandalos

Overview

As massive as casino resorts have recently become, the casino floor where the actual gambling takes place is always a space-limited area. Just as a casino resort only has a set number of hotel rooms, it too only has limited square footage to incorporate its sports book, slot and video poker machines, and gaming tables, whether they are for blackjack, poker, roulette, craps, pai gow, or any other gambling game. This means that it is imperative for casino operators to utilize the casino floor to its maximum potential. Today's software solutions can help casino operators reduce waiting times at restaurants, at the poker tables or at check-in. Other solutions allow slot players to find the location of their favorite slot machines on a floor plan on the casino's website so they can map out their path before they reach the casino floor. In this chapter, I will discuss the solutions currently available to casino operators as well as the products that are in the development stage and will be coming to a casino floor in the not too distant future.

A 24-Hour Sports Book

The sports book is perhaps the most under-utilized area of a casino. Compared to the enormous amounts of gambling variety available on the Internet, sports books in the U.S. offer a dearth of options for the gambler. For example, on betfair.com, gamblers can not only make a bet but he or she can also lay a bet[19]. There is no reason why the sports book can't be as busy — or busier — than the poker and craps table in the wee hours of the morning.

Starting in Australia, then moving onto Japan, Dubai, Europe, then the East Coast tracks in the United States and finally onto the tracks in California, horse racing is practically a 24-hour sport. When the lights dim at the Los Alamitos racetrack in California, horses are being led to the starting gate in Melbourne Park, Australia, and Happy Valley, Hong Kong.

In Hong Kong, the horse racing industry is a $12 billion yearly business. In his book *Telling Lies and Getting Paid*, Michael Konik writes that in Hong Kong, a city of 6 million people, 750,000 people have telephone betting accounts, and one million people place bets every racing day at any of 125 off-track outlets. Casino operators in the U.S. could cater to these customers and fill up a section of the casino that is normally pretty vacant between the hours of 11 pm and 6 am EST.

Mobile Check-In

In June 2008, Delta Air Lines teamed up with the Transportation Security Administration (TSA) to let travelers check-in to flights using their mobile phones. Delta gave customers the option to use their mobile devices to

---

[19] A bet backing something that won't happen (usually the casino's or house's position).

check-in and receive an electronic boarding pass. At security checkpoints, the TSA scans the electronic boarding pass, checks the customer's ID and processes the customer through security. At the departure gate, these passengers present their electronic boarding pass to the gate agent and board as normal. Delta sees future enhancements that could include upgrades from standby and same-day, round-trip check-in on delta.com[20].

Omni Hotels has also launched a mobile web site to improve the way it manages CRM as well as increase revenue through reservations. Omni Hotel guests can book reservations, get hotel information, download special offers or check-in from their Internet-enabled handsets. In future, Omni Hotels could allow guests to request valet service, housekeeping, or to make requests from the hotel during their stay[21].

Marketing at the Slot Machine

IGT's Service Window technology allows casino operators to market directly to a player from a slot machine. Basically, a casino can communicate directly with a player at key moments in their play, such as when a player is buying in, cashing out, or enjoying a big win. Offers could include promotions for a return visit, a free play coupon, or dinner or drinks at an on-site restaurant or bar. It is a great, cost effective way to reach to a player. Service Window games should appear at MGM Mirage's City Center project by the end of 2009[22].

---

[20] http://blog.delta.com/2008/06/24/paperless-mobile-check-in-goes-live-at-laguardia/ (Accessed March 1, 2009).
[21] http://www.omnihotels.com/Home/AboutOmniHotels/Press/PressReleases/080110PressRelease.aspx (Accessed March 1, 2009).
[22] Green, Marian. Marketing at the Slot Machine. *Casino Journal*. February 2009. Volume 22, Number 2.

No More Standing In Line For a Table

One of the most important things a casino operator must do is keep their patrons spending money, whether that is by gambling or purchasing other offerings at the property such as food, spa services, or retail merchandise. Casino operators can incorporate software systems that send voice calls and text messages to a customer's cell phones so they're free to roam as far as their cell coverage will take them. Compared to restaurant coaster pager systems, which usually have a limited range, these systems will allow customers who make a reservation the freedom to either venture onto the casino floor to continue gambling or to head to a store to spend their money in one of the hotel's retail establishments. The system can even take reservations in poker rooms when the tables are filled so poker players don't have to stand around waiting for a spot to open up.

Server Based Gaming

Server based gaming is a solution employed by casinos and video lotteries to operate electronic gaming machines and video lottery terminals, the former commonly referred to as slot machines. A server based gaming system includes a central system and gaming terminals, which connect to the central system. The system may be operated locally over a Local Area Network (LAN) or span large geographical areas, even entire nations, over a Wide Area Network (WAN) such as the Internet.

Slot Search

On their website, Boyd Gaming allows customers to view a map of the location of every one of their slot machines. It's a great use of resources because it cuts down on the time an individual needs to find their preferred gambling venue and any time you cut down on the time it takes a gambler to find his or her preferred game there is a corresponding increase in the time they have to gamble.

Conclusion

The most important thing for a casino operator to do is to get a player onto the floor so that he or she can gamble. The next most important thing is to maximize the profit potential of the property. The software solutions discussed in this chapter, along many other solutions that are only in the development stage right now will go a long way to increasing a casino operator's profitability.

CHAPTER EIGHT

THE ASIAN GAMBLER

> *"Macau is not a territory with a casino company, but a casino company with a territory."*
> ~Joke heard throughout Macau

Overview

Every casino operator should have an understanding and appreciation for the Asian gambler since they are probably the biggest gamblers in the world. Amongst all Asians, the Chinese are almost certainly the biggest gamblers of all. Gambling has been deeply ingrained in the Chinese culture for thousands of years. The Chinese New Year greeting, "Gong hei fat choy" literally means, "wishing you good fortunes and wealth." Many Chinese believe in the mystical qualities of luck, fate and chance. For whatever reason they do it, Asian gamblers in general, and Chinese gamblers in particular, will be a major force in the coming decades. In 2006, over 10 billion dollars was wagered on the World Cup soccer finals. 60 percent of those bets came from mainland China and Southeast Asia[23], which is an amazing figure when one considers the average salary of a Chinese person is about $1,700 per year. In this chapter, I will discuss the culture of Asian gamblers, what they like and what they dislike so that a casino operator can attain a basic understanding of how to cater to this valuable customer.

Las Vegas is a favorite destination for Chinese and Asian gamblers. Some casino executives estimate that 80 percent of Las Vegas' high rollers come from China, Taiwan or Japan. This has obviously not

---

[23] www.people.com.cn (accessed March 1, 2009)

gone unnoticed by the casino industry, as several casinos have redesigned large sections of their casino floors to cater to these Asian players. Specifically, Caesars Palace and Trump Taj Mahal have installed imported carved wood baccarat tables and several pai gow poker tables. Specifically because of these Asian gamblers, baccarat now generates far more revenue than roulette or craps[24]. Asian gamblers tend to spend much more of their disposable income on gambling than their Asian-American counterparts and they are therefore coveted by casino operators.

After Portugal returned Macau to China in 1999 after 440 years of colonial rule, gambling grew into a huge and enormously profitable industry. Last year 22 million visitors gambled more that $6.5 billion at Macau's gambling tables, which means that in terms of total revenue Macau is now a bigger gambling destination than Las Vegas. Macau is considerably smaller than Las Vegas but it is one of the most densely populated places on the planet and tables there actually pull in about three times more revenue than they do in Las Vegas[25].

Rolling Chip Programs

Widely popular in Macau, rolling chip programs have recently been introduced to the United States by Foxwoods Resort Casino in Connecticut. Rolling chip programs allow patrons to purchase non-negotiable gaming chips with a 1.5 percent rebate at the time of purchase. The customer then uses the non-negotiable chips while betting during play. His or her winning bets are then paid out with regular cash chips while the

---

[24] http://travel.nytimes.com/2007/06/13/business/13vegas.html?pagewanted=print. (Accessed March 1, 2009).
[25] It's a Brawl. China's Gamblers Are the Prize, *The New York Times,* David Barboza, March 25, 2007

house takes losing bets back. Rolling chip programs offer players an instant advance rebate that allows the customer the ability to play longer. Many customers prefer the additional rebate to more traditional complimentary amenities that casinos typically provide.

In Asia, rolling chip programs are very common and usually players use the service of a junket operator. The majority of higher-end table game action comes in through junket operators who often also lease VIP rooms. A normal two- to four-day junket will usually 'roll' their initial deposit six to eight times. The casino's net profit comes from the total win from the group, less all expenses and commission. Once again, the *Theoretical win* formula is in play here. "Rolling" encourages longer casino play, or action; therefore the casino should make more profits.

Chinese Gambling Dos and Don'ts

Casino operators should be aware that the Chinese gambler can be very superstitious and they should be aware of certain dos and don'ts, including the following:

- Do check into a hotel room that has the lucky number 3 or 8 in it.
- When playing baccarat, players should call out *'Ding'* or *'Deng'* before opening the cards.
- Before embarking on a major casino trip, pray or make an offering to the gods.
- Be aware of the numerology of your life as the winning numbers are there to be seen and interpreted.
- Don't speak the word *'books'* when someone is gambling as, in Chinese, it sounds like *'lose.'*

- Never count your winnings or calculate your loses during gambling.
- Avoid the sight of nuns or monks.
- Do wear red underwear or undergarments when gambling.
- Don't hit or touch another person's shoulder while they are gambling.
- For men, refrain from sex before gambling.
- Do enter a casino through a back entrance rather than the main entrance as the front entrance is cursed by the feng shui masters.
- Don't check into hotel rooms with unlucky numbers such as 4 and 14.

Asian Games

Baccarat is the game preferred by most Asian players but casino operators should be aware that there are several other games that are staples in Macau casinos.

Baccarat: Believed to have been introduced into France from Italy during the reign of Charles VIII of France, Baccarat is a game in which cards are dealt to two hands named Player and Banker. A gambler can bet on the Player, the Banker, or on a Tie, or any combination of the three. The object of the game is to correctly pick which hand will have the higher score, with the highest score in Baccarat being 9 and the lowest being 0.

Belankas: This unusual game hails from Java. A four-sided top, marked with a crab, a flower, a fish, and a prawn is spun, and covered with a bowl.

Players place their bets on squares marked with the same images. If you bet on the shape that lands face up when the top has stopped, you win. Belankas is very similar to Fan-Tan in terms of payouts and odds.

Fan-Tan: A traditional pebble-counting game that is commonly found in the casinos of Macau. The game is simple. A square is marked in the centre of an ordinary table, or a square piece of metal is laid on it, with the sides being marked 1, 2, 3 and 4. The banker puts a double handful of small buttons, beads, coins, dried beans, or similar articles on the table, which he covers with a metal bowl, or "tan koi."

The players then bet on the numbers, setting their stakes on the side of the square that bears the number selected. (Players can also bet on the corners, for example between No. 2 and No. 3). When all bets are placed, the bowl is removed, and the "tan kun" or croupier uses a small bamboo stick to remove the buttons from the heap, four at a time, until the final batch is reached. If it contains four buttons, the backer of No. 4 wins; if three, the backer of No. 3 wins, and so on. The banker deducts a 5% commission from the stake, and the winner wins three times the amount of his stake thus reduced.

Mah Jong: This classic Chinese gambling game is similar to Rummy, except tiles are used instead of cards. To win, a player must assemble four sets of threes (either three of a kind or a sequence in the same suit) and an extra pair. There are a number of special hands that score higher than the usual amount of points and have exotic names such as "Heavenly Peace," "Moon from the Bottom of the Sea," or "Thirteen Orphans." The game is played differently from country to country, province-to-province, and even household-to-household.

Pai Gow: This game is played with a set of 32 Chinese dominoes that are slightly larger and thicker than American Dominoes. Each player in Pai Gow is dealt a hand of four dominoes, which he must arrange in two pairs, one high and one low. Both of the player's hands must beat the banker's two hands in order to collect. The banker changes with each round, one of the players taking on the house's role each time. The player who becomes the banker must put up a certain amount of money as a bet. All of the competing players can then match his bet. If the banker wins, he can collect a great deal, but if he loses, he must pay off all the bet against him, which can be substantial.

Sic Bo: Of ancient Chinese origin, this classic dice game, also known as Tai Sai, Dai Siu, big and small or hi-lo, is played with three dice. In Sic Bo, three dice are shaken in a cup and placed hidden under the cup on the table. Bets are made. The simple bet is high or low. Low is when the sum of the dice is less than 10, high when it is greater. Winning this kind of bet pays 1 to 1. Guessing the actual numbers thrown make for much higher payoffs.

Conclusion

The Asian culture is more suited for gambling than any other culture in the world. Many casino operators in Las Vegas actively court the Asian gambler but they should learn to embrace them more. First and foremost, casino operators must understand the cultural uniqueness of the Asian gambler; why they are there and what games they prefer to play. For example, in Macau, three percent of a casino's revenue comes from their slot machines while 97 percent comes from table games. Conversely, in

Las Vegas slot revenue is considerably higher than table games revenue. Many casino host special events during the Chinese New Year because it, along with the western New Year and the NFL's Super Bowl weekend rank as the three busiest times for Las Vegas casinos[26].

---

[26] http://www.reuters.com/article/marketsNews/idINN2325581220090123?rpc=44 (Accessed March 1, 2009)

CHAPTER NINE

A COMPREHENSIVE SOLUTION

"You don't close a sale, you open a relationship if you want to build a long-term, successful enterprise."
~Patricia Fripp

Overview

A successful solution must enable an improved customer experience because it allows users to set up a framework that captures and intelligently manages the collected customer data. It must also provide access to property-wide patron information while allowing users to generate strategic marketing campaign initiatives that improve the utilization of information in the following ways:

- Consolidates disparate gaming and non-gaming information for a comprehensive patron view.
- Consolidates data from the various patron touch point source systems to create a centralized data repository of information. These source systems can include IGT Advantage (Gaming), Agilysys LMS (Hotel), InfoGenesis (Retail) and SpaSoft (Spa).
- Implements a nightly production process to automate a batch update of the data warehouse controlled through a Data Integration interface.
- Contains an Enterprise Business Intelligence platform for information that distributes through a variety of channels, including a web-enabled executive dashboard,

interactive (OLAP) reporting, static reporting, as well as desktop functionality through the add-ins for MS Office and several other systems.
- By using advanced analytics to apply statistical methods to the patron data, it allows data mining and predictive analytics that can help in the modeling and segmentation that is required for more targeted and effective marketing initiatives.
- Centralizes control of the marketing campaign creation and management process that is integrated with the analytic and business intelligence environments.
- Models, reports and analyzes patron information.
- Automates and personalizes marketing campaigns.

All of these tools should help a casino operator to optimize the casino's resources by putting their most profitable patrons in their hotel, on their casino floor, or at their events and property – ultimately maximizing their revenue.

Patron Data Quality and Integration

Unless a casino operator creates a single source for patron information, they can spend a great deal of time trying to match people from different systems. A patron data quality and integration function brings gaming and non-gaming data together from different sources to create a total patron view for segmentation purposes. Patron ID data is not always collected from different systems for a variety of reasons: perhaps the data is not required, maybe there is no place to enter the data, or possibly there is no incentive for a player to use their player card. Whatever the issue, an intelligent gaming solution will allow for this data to be captured, cleansed and consolidated, ensuring the best possible holistic and complete view of the patron.

Patron Value

This measures, analyzes and reports on total patron value; i.e., the amount a single patron spends at the casino property or properties, whether it is money spent in the hotel, at the spa, on entertainment or on any other activity that a casino wishes to measure. This helps provide a more accurate assessment of what a casino's patrons are ultimately worth to the property.

Patron Segmentation

Patron segmentation divides patrons by customer worth, booking trends, behavioral factors and other relevant business patterns. A user can see a total guest view for more effective business insight, including a guest's preferences, as well as the likelihood of guests to respond to promotions and travel trends.

Patron Predictive Modeling

Perhaps the most important analytic feature is the patron predictive modeling function. A casino can build models that predict patron frequency while calculating their individual worth into the future. Historical data may show how often a customer visits a casino but predictive models reveal which customers are likely to visit other casinos in the market as well. Once a customer is identified, they can be targeted with campaigns that attempt to increase their loyalty. This enables the casino to have more profitable marketing campaigns. Predictions can also be customized for each regional market, which is important because frequent customers in one city can look quite different from frequent customers in another city.

Patron Revenue Forecasting

Patron revenue forecasting accurately forecasts future unconstrained and constrained room demand, retention rate, price elasticity and dilution by customer segment. This includes forecasting cancellations, no-shows and staffing needs as well as optimizing resources needed to properly serve the forecasted patron demand.

Total Guest View

This process integrates guest interactions into a single data warehouse that creates a true value for each guest. This combines transactions from each operational system: player tracking, slot games, table games, hotel, point-of-sale systems, retail, and food and beverage. This approach reduces the impact on the operational system performance for report generation and analysis. The solutions provide a unified view of guests across the enterprise that incorporates information from all touch points and channels, ensuring that customer information is consistent, secure, accurate and comprehensible to users.

Guest Intelligence

Guest intelligence provides the following benefits:

- **Targeted Guest Marketing Strategies**: Utilizing advanced analytic techniques, a casino operator will have the tools to be able to conduct targeted marketing campaigns using proven statistical techniques in a user-friendly manner.
- **Manage Marketing Effectiveness:** The system will allow casino operators to better understand the results and effectiveness of the marketing campaigns and promotions plus how they affect the financial bottom line.
- **Media Optimization**: A casino operator will be able to fully understand how to optimize their media expenditures and maximize their reach to their target markets. This system allows the casino operator to effectively increase revenue per advertising dollar spent by optimizing various media channels.
- **Contact Management**: Contact Management enables the casino operator to analyze, manage, and optimize the time, frequency, and message specifics of guest communications.
- **Web channel effectiveness**: Web Analytics enables the casino operator to be proactive in reaching out to customers online. With it, the casino operator can quickly and precisely segment customers and then apply rules-based engines to link specific offers with chosen segments providing a more personalized customer experience. This can lead to immediate increases in

customer satisfaction and Web bookings. Over the long term, guest retention rates and lifetime guest value also rise.

Query & Analysis

The solution must provide multiple query interfaces for differing skill levels, thereby enabling information producers to access and query data on their own without having to learn new skills. The system must access a multitude of data sources (at least five at any given property) and have inter-operability to query across multiple databases and platforms. Without this multi-vendor architecture it is difficult if not impossible to build a comprehensive data warehouse to support any valuable query and analysis function.

OLAP Analysis

This allows users to analyze summary data organized along business dimensions. Business intelligence integrates OLAP data storage and navigation into the reporting environment. An Enterprise BI Server should provide a powerful multi-dimensional database that is designed to provide fast, easy access to large volumes of summarized data. A web-based data exploration interface lets users look at large volumes of data quickly from multiple angles. Users can then get high-level views of data, as well as views with an increasing level of detail.

Visualization

An extensive suite of graphical data presentation options can be included for business and scientific use. These graphics can be produced as reports that can be surfaced in the portal or as part of an application, or as a freestanding graphic. Charts and plots can be created and delivered on hundreds of different devices. Users can also create and integrate geographic maps within the OLAP application as an interactive data exploration interface.

Integrated Analytics

This can include analytic results or the ability to include and run analytic models directly from within their BI interface of choice, whether that is a web browser or Microsoft Excel. Analytic algorithms can be of the highest quality in the industry, ensuring accuracy and precision for greater certainty and confidence in results.

Deliverables

The reporting and analysis needs of a casino include a wide array of deliverables in several different formats. These deliverables can utilize an information delivery portal and interactive web environment for the distribution of the information. The portal can provide a mechanism to deliver an executive dashboard with the initial key performance indicators and a variety of reporting/analytic deliverables. There will be custom reports tailored for each of the primary data sources for IGT, Bally, LMS,

InfoGenesis and SpaSoft along with a flash report to monitor overall property revenue for the previous day. These report deliverables will assist with the Q/A process for data validation in the data warehouse and can include one or more of the following custom reports that can assist with management and marketing analysis:

1. Average Daily Worth (Quality of Player)
2. Miles Traveled to Property (Geographic Penetration)
3. Top Metropolitan Statistical Area (MSA) (Key Urban Areas & Population Centers)
4. Months Known Locally (Length of Guest's Relationship at Property)
5. Age of Guest (Life Stage of Guest)
6. Slots vs. Table Players by Average Daily Worth
7. Slots vs. Table Players by Number of Month's Known
8. Slots vs. Table Players by Age of Guest
9. Known Hotel Status by Average Daily Worth
10. Known Hotel Status by Miles Traveled
11. Known Hotel Guests Only by Miles Traveled by Average Daily Worth
12. Current Tier Card Level by Game Type Played
13. Current Tier Card Level by Average Daily Worth Level
14. VIP Guests Only by Game Type by Months Known
15. New vs. Existing Player by Average Daily Worth (Quality of Sign-ups)
16. New vs. Existing Player by Distance

17. All MSA's

Internet Gambling

Some experts contend that we are as early in the evolution of the Internet as the Kitty Hawk was in the evolution of the airplane. With the Internet, the possibilities are truly endless. The Internet is the most interactive and consumer measurable medium ever created.

A recent Price Waterhouse Coopers study concluded that if two online gambling bills that were recently defeated in the U.S. legislature had passed, the federal government would have reaped a windfall of at least $17.6 billion in taxes over the ensuing ten years[27]. These bills — Representative Barney Frank's (D-MA) Internet Gambling Regulation and Enforcement Act of 2007 and Representative Jim McDermott's (D-WA) Internet Gambling Regulation and Tax Enforcement Act — were cleared from the books at the end of 2007, but the troubled state of the U.S. economy in 2009 will certainly have politicians looking at additional ways to generate revenue. We've seen this on the state level, where many states such as Louisiana, Mississippi, and Florida, among many others, have chosen to legalize gambling in order to close budget gaps. I believe it's only a matter of time before the federal government follows suit.

The taxes generated from an Internet bill wouldn't require any new taxes. Instead, the government would tax winnings and add a wagering tax. Estimated revenues range from a low of $8.7 billion to a high of $17.6 billion assuming that all states that currently allow land-based gambling would allow online gambling. If all the ten states that currently restrict online gambling — Illinois, Indiana, Louisiana, Michigan, Nevada, New

---

[27] http://pokeronamac.com/news/study-reveals-us-could-make-billions-in-online-gambling-taxes/ (accessed March 1, 2009)

Jersey, New York, Oregon, South Dakota, and Washington — repeal their prohibition laws, online gambling revenue would rise to $33.9 billion. If sports wagering was included and all states that currently allow land-based casinos allowed sports wagering, tax revenues would rise another $10.2 billion. If the ten states that don't allow online gambling were to be included, tax revenues would rise by over $21.4 billion[28].

On September 26, 2008, Sen. Robert Menendez (D-NJ) submitted the Internet Skill Game Licensing and Control Act to the U.S. Senate. If enacted, this bill will allow the licensing of Internet skill game facilities, which includes poker. Defining poker as a game of skill is an important distinction because, like poker, bridge and mah jong, a player's success is directly related to his skill level. Since sports betting doesn't qualify as a game of skill, the bill still bans sports betting but the Internet Skill Game Licensing and Control Act would help clarify online poker's legality.

Coupled with a faltering economy and the Democratic landslide victory in the 2008 election cycle, the current political climate has become much more favorable to Internet gambling. Only the Koran strictly forbids gambling thereby making it a sin, but there is nothing in the Bible that says gambling is a sin yet that hasn't stopped many opportunistic politicians to blame some of society's ills on the gambling industry. Casino operators should be aware of the great potential the Internet holds. Should the bill pass, poker tournaments could be held on line, with players betting on the hands of the pros.

Conclusion

Unlike the infamous Roman Emperor Caligula — a notorious cheater and

---

[28] http://pokeronamac.com/news/study-reveals-us-could-make-billions-in-online-gambling-taxes/ (accessed March 1, 2009)

the worst kind of loser — today's casino operators can't execute those who beat them at the gaming tables. They can, however, ensure that their winning — and losing — patrons return to the casino by marketing to them correctly, which means marketing directly to their needs, wants and expectations. Casino operators are faced with the daily challenge of how to fill the thousands of rooms in their hotels, the hundred or so gaming tables on the casino floor and the thousands of seats in their entertainment venues. It's an enormous task and a task that would be impossible without the software tools currently available to them. Today, with available revenue management tools, casinos can ensure that not one seat at the gaming tables goes to waste, even if it is sitting empty.

This book was written to help casino operators envision the casino floor of the twenty-first century, a floor where computers provide analytics that track players, fill seats, catch cheats, and market directly to the patrons, among many, many other things. It is a brave new world of gambling, a world where, hopefully, the casino operator can develop an understanding of their patron unheard of in any the previous century. It is an understanding that brings the patron experience to new levels of customer service and that will, hopefully, keep guests coming back year after year after year.

GLOSSARY

Actual Win/Loss - The actual amount of money won or lost by a player. Compare this with ***Theoretical Win*** defined below.

Analytics - the study of business data using statistical analysis in order to discover and understand historical patterns in order to predict and improve future business performance.

Carousel – A collection of machines that may have a common jackpot linked together via fiber-optic cables in one specific area or location.

Casino Advantage - The edge that the House (casino) has over the players.

Casino Rate - A reduced hotel-room rate (price) that the casinos offer to good customers.

Club Kiosk - An ATM-style device that allows players to access their points and promotional award accounts in order to convert balances directly to complementaries and vouchers. Depending on configuration, the club kiosk may also perform loyalty-marketing duties by conveying merchandising and advertising messages.

Comps - A Complimentary — or Comp for short — is a free item the casino provides to the player based on their play. These can include just about anything depending on how much the player gambles, but it generally includes free rooms and meals. Many casinos set comp policies by giving the player back a set percentage of their earning potential. Although comp and rebate policies based on theoretical loss are the most popular, rebates on actual losses and dead chip programs are also used in some casinos.

Comps serve as an effective marketing tool for casinos. Their intent is to provide publicity for the property in attracting the "right" type of customers. Experts believe that people receiving comps feel an obligation to gamble at the comping property because of enhanced customer loyalty. However, a New Jersey study tracking rated players found that seven of 10 players changed their casino loyalty despite having received comps. Certainly, the objective of comps is to reward customer patronage, while at the same time maintain an acceptable profit level. The risk of comping too much (overcomping) is that bad customers are encouraged to return to the casino, while the risk of comping too little (undercomping) is that good players may be alienated and their patronage lost. Both of these problems are very costly. So, ideally, a casino will comp at a level necessary to attract and reward good customers, but not retain bad customers.

Customer Relationship Management (CRM) - A strategy used to learn more about customers' needs and behaviors in order to develop stronger relationships with them and create a value exchange on both sides. Software used to capture preferences and implement customer loyalty strategies.

Double Down - On his first two cards, the player may "double down," i.e., "double" his bet and receive only one card face "down." To do this he moves a second bet equal to the first into the betting box next to his original bet.

ePromo – A promotional marketed offer either delivered by email or downloadable from a website.

Earning Potential – See *Theoretical Win*

Expected Win Rate - In slot machines, the percentage on the total amount of money wagered that you can expect to win back over time.

Game Volatility - A measure of the variation of the actual hold from the theoretical hold as well as the dispersion of pay amounts in a game. A game's volatility can fall into one of three categories: High, Medium, and Low.

Meters - Slot machines utilize both mechanical (hard) and software meters to collect game play data. Hardware meters collect lifetime totals and cannot be reset. Software meters are displayed in the statistical data mode, and can be reset to zero.

Metropolitan Statistical Area (MSA) -The general concept of an MSA is that of a core area containing a large population nucleus, together with adjacent communities having a high degree of economic and social integration with that core. For example the Chattanooga, TN, MSA not only contains the 4 counties in Tennessee nearest to Chattanooga, but also contains the 3 North Georgia counties that are just across the state line.

Player Tracking System (PTS) - A data collection package that enables the casino owner/operator to identify and gather information about players via ID cards and readers.

Point Of Sale System (POS) - A computerized system that retail outlets such as restaurants, gift shops, etc, enter orders and maintain various accounting information. It generally interfaces with the Property Management System.

Points - Many casinos offer players a comp point program, as part of their player club, in which points are awarded for every bet the player makes in the casino. Generally, one comp point is awarded for every $10 wagered. These comp points can then be converted to cash usually at a rate of $1 for every 100 comp points accumulated. Some casinos also let players purchase items in the retail shops with points or even use their points to "purchase" tickets for a giveaway drawing for a car or boat. Comp points also serve as a valuable tool in tracking your wager requirement (WR), as you can see how much you have wagered by the amount of comp points you have.

Property Management System (PMS) - A computerized front desk system that manages hotel room inventory, guest billing and interfaces with various other systems such as telephone, call accounting, point of sale (POS), entertainment, etc.

Racino - A combined race track and casino. In some cases, the gambling is limited to slot machines, but many locations are beginning to include table games such as blackjack, poker and roulette.

Revenue Management System (RMS) - The software application hotels use to control the supply and price of their inventory in order to achieve maximum revenue or profit, by managing availability, room types, stay patterns (future and historical), etc.

Revenue per Available Room (RevPAR) - A statistic used in the hotel industry used to measure revenue per available room. Total hotel room revenue divided by the total rooms available to rent for a day or range of dates.

Revenue per Occupied Room (RevPOR) - Calculated by taking the total daily revenue (including ancillary revenues) and dividing it by the total number of occupied rooms at the hotel.

RFB - An acronym referring to comped with free *R*oom, *F*ood, and *B*everages.

Radio Frequency Identification (RFID) technology -

Server-Based Gaming - A system that provides for the high-speed delivery of game content, game configurations, and direct player marketing. The downloaded game content is played on the machine and the machine determines the result. The system may also allow for the downloading of software updates, such as customer notifications, and also can be used to update peripheral software like bill acceptors, ticket printers, etc.

Theoretical Win or **Theo** - Represents the amount the casino will keep in the long run and is the best representation of the actual value of a player. It signifies what should have happened statistically speaking. Theoretical win is calculated by multiplying together four variables: average bet, time played, decisions per hour and house advantage.

REFERENCES

Gilbert, Alorie. 2005. Vegas casino bets on RFID. ZDNet News, February 9. http://news.zdnet.com/2100-1009_22-141181.html (accessed March 1, 2009).

Karoul, Steve & Macomber, Dean. How a Professional Casino Consultant Can Help 'Optimize' Your Casino Marketing Plan. http://euroasiacasino.com

Kilby, Jim, and Fox, Jim. 1998. Casino operations management. New York: John Wiley. January 28, 1998.

Krigman, Alan. 1995. Don't let an increased table limit force you to bet too high. http://krigman.casinocitytimes.com/articles/5265.html.

Peister, Clayton. 2007. Table-games revenue management: Applying survival analysis. *Cornell Hotel and Restaurant Administration Quarterly*. Volume 48, Issue 1 70-87

Sturgeon, Will. 2005. Technology can't beat casino cheaters: RFID, optical scanning, facial recognition...? 'Bring it on'...." *http://www.silicon.com/research/specialreports/gambling/0,3800010160,39153954,00.htm*.

Reith, Gerda. 2002. *The Age of Chance, Gambling in Western Culture*. Routledge.

Thelen, Shawn, Mottner, Sandra and Berman, Barry, 2004. Data Mining: On the Trail to Marketing Gold, *Business Horizons*, (November-December)

Wyld, David. 2008. Radio frequency identification: Advance intelligence for table games in casinos. *Cornell Hospitality Quarterly*. 49 (May): 134-144

Wyld, David. 2005. Playing with the house's money: Casinos are betting big on RFID to improve their abilities to track table play and deliver better customer service. *Global Identification*. 20 (May): 20-27

Yeoman, Ian, and Ingold, Anthony. 1997. In Yield management:

Strategies for the service industries, ed. *Decisionmaking*. Ian Yeoman and Anthony Ingold. London: Cassell.

Zeni, Richard H. 2001. Improved forecast accuracy in airline revenue management by unconstraining estimates from censored data. Ph.D. diss., Rutgers University, New Brunswick, NJ.

ABOUT THE AUTHOR

Clive Pearson

Clive was born in Pakistan, grew up in Singapore, and was educated in England. Clive earned his Bachelor of Science degree with a minor in finance from Clemson University. In 1983, he started his first technology company Creative Programming, Inc., to develop inventory control systems. In the early 1990s, Clive developed software for the top-secret nuclear class submarine the USS Seawolf.

In 1995, he founded Qualex Consulting Services. In the last ten years, Clive has been consulting in business intelligence, data modeling and integration for strategic gaming and hospitality organizations. Clive's leadership has been instrumental in the implementation of business solutions for Paragon Casino, Valley View Casino, Pearl River Resorts, Foxwoods Casino, Hard Rock Las Vegas, and Delaware Park, among others. Qualex has won awards for its Quality and Excellence for which it was founded upon. Qualex qualified as a SAS Gold Partner in 2002 and has been honored with both the prestigious SAS Partner Excellence - Field's Choice Award, as well as the coveted Partner Excellence Award. Clive's knowledge of patron needs combined with strategic direction for hospitality and gaming is at the core of Qualex's philosophy and success.

INDEX

2D bar code, 59
4510 Touch ID Terminal, 36
Accelerated betting strategy, 69
ACSC™, 33
Actual win, 16
Actual win/loss, 15, 110
Advanced analytic techniques, 13
Advantage, 15, 97
Agilysys, 31, 37, 97
Analytics, 16, 98
Aristocrat, 32
Artificial neural networks, 18
Asian gambler, 89, 90, 95
AT&T, 59
Automating campaigns, 47
Awareness, 44
Baccarat, 15, 90, 92, 93
Baez, Joan, 10
Bally, 33
Ballys, 37
Behavioral information, 46
Behavioral patterns, 6
Belankas, 93
Berman, Barry, 116
Birthday Campaigns, 45
Blackberry Storm, 53
Blackjack, 5, 24, 43, 49, 72, 83, 113
Blaise Pascal, 8
Blogs, 49
Boyd Gaming, 87
Business Intelligence, 12
Caesars Palace, 90
Caligula, 108
Card counter, 68, 69, 70, 72
Carousel, 110
Casino Advantage, 110
Casino floor, 83
Casino marketing, 7, 40, 49
Casino Rate, 110
Central reservation systems, 29
Chip validation, 67
CHIPCO International, 67
Churchill, Winston, 40
Click to Call, 59
Club Kiosk, 110
CMP™, 34
CMS/400™, 33
Coaster pager systems, 86

Comp, 113
Comprehensive patron view, 97
Comps, 16, 66, 67, 73, 110, 111
Contact management, 102
Counterfeiting, 67, 70
Coupon codes, 45, 57
Coupons, 45
Craps, 83, 84, 90
Cross-selling, 22
Crystal Report Writer, 31
Customer analytics, 20
Customer behavior, 12, 20, 22, 76
Customer data, 6, 17, 23, 97
Customer experience, 5
Customer loyalty program, 11, 56
Customer Relationship Management, 10, 11, 12, 48, 85, 111
Customer retention, 25
Customer segments, 40
Customer's behavior, 20
Customer's value, 20, 42
Dandalos, Nicholas (Nick the Greek), 83
Data integration, 16, 21, 98
Data Integration interface., 98
Data marts, 30
Data mining, 17, 18, 19, 21, 26, 98
Data repository, 97
Data sets, 17
Data sources, 30, 31, 103
Data warehouse, 30, 31, 98, 101, 103
DB2, 37
Dead chip programs, 111
Dealer cheating, 68
Decision trees, 18
Deliverables, 104
Delta Air Lines, 84
Demand based pricing, 77
Demand creation, 43, 44
Discount codes, 60
Double Down, 111
Earning Potential, 112
Educational downloads, 59
Enriquez, John, 23, 24, 25
Enterprise Business Intelligence, 98
Enterprise Systems, 28
ePromo, 111
Expected win rate, 112

EZ Pay® Ticketing, 35
Facebook, 48, 49
Fan-Tan, 93
Fast Eddie Felson, 7
Feeder markets, 41
Fox, Jim, 116
Frequent player programs, 14
Fripp, Patricia, 97
G1 Android, 53
Gambling addiction, 71
Gambling strategies, 73
Gaming Partners International, 64, 67
General User Interface, 30
Genetic algorithms, 18
Gilbert, Alorie, 116
Godin, Seth, 53
Guest bookings, 28
Guest intelligence, 13, 101
Guest knowledge, 23
Guest preferences, 23
Guest spend, 13
Harrah's, 14, 25, 56, 60
High rollers, 16, 66, 90
Hooey, Bob, 76
Hotel fill rates, 13
House advantage, 15
Identification Friend or Foe, 64
IGT, 37, 97
IGT Advantage Bonusing™, 35
IGT Advantage System, 34
Incentives, 44
InfoGenesis, 97
Information Delivery Portal, 30
Ingold, Anthony, 76, 117
Integrated analytics, 104
Interactive web, 30
Internet, 6, 58, 62, 72, 84, 85, 106, 107
Internet Gambling, 106
Internet Gambling Regulation and Tax Enforcement Act, 106
Internet Skill Game Licensing and Control Act, 107
iPhone, 53, 55, 69
iSeries Gaming, 36
iSeries Leave, 36
iSeries Scheduler, 36
iSeries Timekeeper, 36
Karoul, Steve, 41, 42, 43, 44, 116
Keller, Dr. Matt H., 76
Kilby, Jim, 116
Konik, Michael, 84
Krigman, Alan, 76, 116

Kronos, 36, 37
Las Vegas, 3, 4, 60, 77, 90, 95
Lift and gains charts, 46
LMS, 97
Lodging Management System®, 31
Long range transponder system, 64
Macau, 3, 64, 89, 90, 93
Macomber, Dean, 41, 42, 43, 44, 116
Mah Jong, 94
Market segmentation, 41, 42, 43
Marketing automation, 45, 50
Marketing campaigns, 4, 7, 13, 16, 20, 24, 43, 44, 45, 46, 47, 62, 97, 98, 100, 101, 102
Marketing cycle, 43
Marketing objective, 43
Marketing segmentation, 45
MCC™, 34
Media Optimization, 102
Microblogs, 48, 49
Micros, 36, 37
Microsoft SQL Server, 31
Minimum wagers, 80
Mobile Analytics, 61, 81
Mobile Check-In, 84
Mobile couponing, 56
Mobile coupons, 57
Mobile Data Access™, 35
Mobile Loyalty, 60
Mobile marketing, 5, 50, 53, 54, 56, 57, 60, 62
Mobile Marketing Association, 54
Mobile marketing campaign, 61
Mobile marketing campaigns, 57
Mobile traffic, 61
Mobile web analytics, 61
Mobile web technology, 53
Model development, 47
Modeling, 22, 98
Monthly Direct Mail, 44
Mottner, Sandra, 116
Multiple regression, 18
MySpace, 48, 49
Nearest neighbor method, 18
Negative bias, 79
Neural networks, 18
Nevada State Gaming Control, 69
Newman, Paul, 7
Nike, 59
OLAP, 98, 103, 104
OLAP Analysis, 103
Omni Hotels, 85

Online communities, 48
Online reservations, 28
OPERA Property Management System, 37
Operational reporting, 31
Oracle, 36, 37
Page views, 61
Pai Gow, 83, 90, 94
Partial sales, 80
Pastposting, 68
Patron ID data, 99
Patron Predictive Modeling, 100
Patron revenue forecasting, 100
Patron Segmentation, 100
patron touch point, 97
Patron value, 67, 99
Pearl River Resort, 23, 24, 25
Pearl River Rewards program, 25
Pearson, Clive, 120
Peister, Clayton, 77, 78, 79, 116
Perks, 25, 66
Pit boss, 76
Pit bosses, 69, 78, 80
Player behavior, 13, 68
Player card, 99
Player card program, 44
Player cards, 12, 19, 20
Player Management System, 15, 16
Player ratings, 67
Player tracking, 14, 16, 28, 67, 101, 112
Player's spend, 44
Point Of Sale System, 112
Point-of-Sale, 14, 101
Point-of-Sales Systems, 29, 101
Points, 113
Poker, 23, 24, 59, 64, 72, 83, 84, 86, 90, 107, 113
Poker tournaments, 45
Post-visit surveys, 21
Predict patron frequency, 22, 100
Predictive analytic solution, 23
Predictive analytics, 4, 17, 20, 21, 22, 25, 26, 77, 80, 98
Predictive insight, 23
Predictive modeling, 46, 47, 100
Predictive models, 20, 46, 100
Progressive Gaming, 64, 67
Promotional Marketing Campaigns, 45
Promotions, 7, 12, 13, 40, 60, 100, 102

Property Management System, 7, 10, 28, 29, 81, 112, 113
Property revenue streams, 13
Radio Frequency Identification, 5, 64, 65, 66, 67, 68, 69, 70, 71, 72, 73, 114
Radio-frequency identification, 28
Reith, Gerda, 116
Repeated visitation, 44
Response data, 47
Response rates, 47, 50
Responsible gaming, 71
Revenue Management, 76, 77, 79, 81, 113
Revenue per available room, 113
Revenue per occupied room, 113
Reward programs, 14
Rewards, 14
RFID chips, 64, 67, 71, 80
RFID-based table-monitoring systems, 68
RFID-embedded chips, 69
Ring leader, 42
Rio, 60
Rolling chip program, 91
Roulette, 68, 83, 90, 113
Rule induction, 18
Segmentation, 98
Segmentation methods, 46
Server based gaming, 86, 114
Service Window, 85, 86
Short Message Service, 53, 54, 55, 59
Sic Bo, 94
Slot machines, 23, 66, 83, 86, 87, 95, 112, 113
Slot player tracking, 10
Slot Search, 87
Slots, 12, 14, 105
Smart card, 72
SMS, 53
SMS Blast, 59
SMS marketing, 5, 56
SMS shortcode, 57
Social media, 49
Social Network, 48
SpaSoft, 37, 97
Sports Book, 84
Spread analyses, 68
SQL/Server, 37
Statistical analysis, 18, 110
Statistical modeling, 17, 19
Sturgeon, Will, 116
Sybase, 37

Table games, 6, 12, 14, 23, 35, 36, 66, 76, 77, 78, 79, 95, 101, 113, 116
Table games management, 76
Table iD™, 35
Table minimum wagers, 76
Table minimums, 6, 77, 80
Table-games revenue management, 6, 76, 77, 78, 80
TableView™, 34
Target market, 44
Targeted Guest Marketing Strategies, 101
Telemarketers, 22
Telemarketing, 21
Teradata, 37
Texting Important People, 56
The Color of Money, 7
Thelan, Shawn, 116
Theo. *See* Theoretical Win
Theoretical loss, 110
Theoretical Win, 15, 41, 91, 110, 112, 114
Third screen, 53
Ticket-in/ticket-out, 28
Total guest value, 13
Total guest view, 101
Total patron value, 99
Total patron view, 99

Total Rewards, 14, 15, 56, 60
Trial offer, 44
Trigger phrases, 22
True count, 70
Trump Taj Mahal, 90
Twitter, 48, 49
Txt2Win, 58
Up-selling, 22
Verizon Wireless, 59
Visual One PMS, 31
Visual Slot Performance™, 35
Vouchers, 110
WAP Push, 58
Weatherford, Lawrence, 79
Web analytics, 102
Web channel effectiveness, 102
Win per available seating hour, 78, 79
Workforce Acquisition, 36
Wyld, David, 65, 66, 69, 72, 116, 117
Yelp, 48
Yelton, Jack, 28
Yeoman, Ian, 76, 117
Yield Management, 76
Yield management systems, 29
Zeni, Richard, 79, 117